The only place w... ...sework comes before sewing ... ...dictionary.

MARY ...

A~Z of Sewing

inspirations books

contents

equipment | the sewing machine

The mechanics of sewing machines are constantly changing with new technology, but the main principles have remained the same. The fabric is moved under the presser foot by the feed dogs below the plate, as the needle passes through the fabric. The correct amount of pressure ensures even feed and will depend on the weight of the fabric being used. Lightweight fabrics require light pressure and vice versa. A walking presser foot is usually available to help with difficult feed problems when stitching suede, vinyl or quilting. Some tasks such as attaching buttons and free motion embroidery do not require feed. Lowering the feed dogs below the stitch plate eliminates the movement.

A sewing machine is a vital piece of equipment for constructing a garment. Look carefully at what is available and choose a machine that best suits your needs. Beginners will require very basic machine features such as straight and zigzag stitches, a well formed buttonhole, some stretch stitches and a small range of embroidery stitches. Familiarise yourself with your machine, studying the instruction manual and attending any workshops offered by the dealer.

Maintenance

Once you have a machine, taking good care of it ensures that it will last a long time. Lint and dust will collect under the base plate and should be removed regularly to keep the machine working smoothly. This is particularly important if sewing velvet, corduroy or other pile fabrics that may shed large amounts of fibre.

Regular oiling will keep the machine working smoothly. Read the manual to determine if, where and how often the machine should be oiled. Have it serviced annually by a qualified mechanic and keep it covered and in a dry place when not in use.

If travelling with your machine, place a soft fabric on the base plate and ensure that the presser foot is down. Computerised machines can be temperamental and may not like being moved at all.

1	electronic panel controls	15	thread tension discs
2	fly wheel	16	take up lever
3	light/power switches	17	pressure dial
4	free arm bed	18	needle position
5	bobbin housing	19	thread holder
6	measuring gauge	20	bobbin winder
7	feed dogs		
8	stitch plate		
9	needle clamp		
10	reverse stitch		
11	stitch speed		
12	needle and housing		
13	presser foot		
14	extension bed		

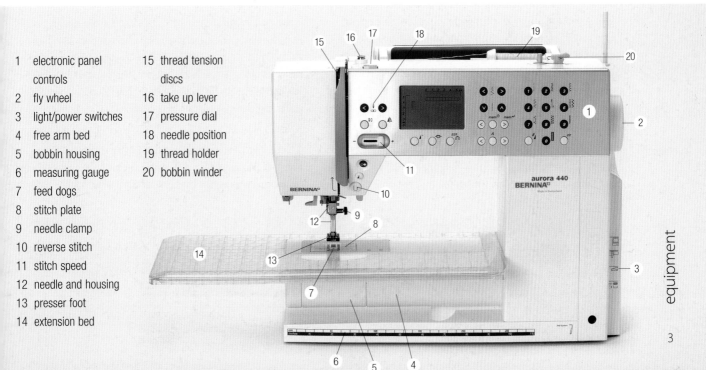

equipment

3

Stitching

Straight stitch is the most used function of a sewing machine. To stitch a seam, the length is usually between 1.5mm - 2.5mm, depending on the fabric being used. The thicker the fabric, the longer the stitch.

Most machines also have a reverse action, used to secure the line of stitching.

Zigzag stitching is defined by stitch length and width and is generally used for neatening seams, appliqué and heirloom sewing. The distance between the diagonal stitches is determined by the stitch length. Stitch width determines how far the needle moves from side to side - the higher the number, the wider the stitch.

Embroidery stitches are pre-programmed zigzag patterns. Modern machines can work an infinite variety of embroidery motifs, using inbuilt digital programs.

Stretch stitches are very strong and suitable for knit fabrics and elastic. They are produced by the needle moving forward or from side to side, while the feed is moving forward and backward. Some stretch stitches are perfect for sewing a seam and neatening at the same time.

Presser feet

Most machines come with a few standard, interchangeable presser feet. An all purpose sewing foot, a zipper foot, an embroidery foot and a buttonhole foot are the most basic, however it is worthwhile investing in others, as each one is designed for a specific purpose. Having the right foot on the machine makes it easier to achieve the best result for the task.

All purpose sewing foot

This is the standard foot for all basic, forward feed sewing. The sole of this foot is flat, providing control as the fabric passes over the feed dogs.

Blind hem foot and edge stitch foot

These feet have a bar running through the centre of the foot in front of the needle. Use the bar as a guide for instances when a line of stitching is required close to a ridge or fold such as hems and for edgestitching or joining two pieces of lace with the edges butted together.

Buttonhole foot

Two grooves under the sole allow the fabric to move freely as the thread builds up to form the end bars of the buttonhole. The guide between the grooves helps keep the side bars parallel and slightly apart.

Cording, piping or beading foot

A large groove in the sole of these feet allows heavier threads, cords and other high relief decorative trims to pass freely under the foot after being stitched as shown on page 143.

Darning foot

A darning foot is spring loaded, hopping over the surface while the fabric is moved from side to side or backwards and forwards. This foot requires the feed dogs to be covered with a special stitch plate or to be lowered under the normal plate.

Embroidery foot

This foot is completely open in front of the needle, making the work clearly visible. There is also a wedge shaped indentation under the foot, which allows dense satin stitching to glide through without becoming jammed. The angle in the indentation makes it possible to follow curves easily.

Pintuck foot

This is used with a twin needle to stitch pintucks, spacing the tucks by positioning the previous tuck in one of the grooves under the foot as shown on page 142.

ZIPPER FOOT

BUTTONHOLE FOOT

EMBROIDERY FOOT

BLIND HEM FOOT

ROLLED HEM FOOT

DARNING FOOT

Rolled hem foot

The raw edge of the fabric is guided through a tunnel in the foot in front of the needle, to produce a perfectly folded and stitched narrow hem.

Zipper foot

This is a narrow, one-toed foot with notches on both sides for the needle positions. Adjust the foot or the needle position to stitch with the required side against the teeth of the zip. A broad foot with rollers that uncurl the zipper chain are available to insert invisible zips.

Accessories

A walking foot works in unison with the lower feed dogs, passing the upper layers of fabric under the foot at the same rate.

The ruffler attachment allows long strips of fabric to be gathered quickly. It is good for soft furnishing projects.

A *spacer bar* and a *blind hem guide* are attachments for presser feet that enable the correct positioning of a line of stitching. A seam or hem guage is fitted into a hole in the bed of the machine. The bar at the end of the guide is then positioned to be a specific distance from the needle.

the overlocker *or serger*

The main purpose of an overlocker is to neaten the raw edges of a seam. Trimming is unnecessary, as the overlocker trims as it sews, using a blade on one side of the stitch plate. It is not intended to be a replacement for a sewing machine.

An overlocker is similar to a sewing machine in that it has a presser foot to control the fabric and a feed system to pass the fabric through. It often uses the same needles. An overlocker has at least two top threads that pass through a needle and two loopers, one upper and one lower, to form interlocking stitches over the raw edge. All the threads are tensioned by passing through discs and thread guides. Each has its own distinct path, often colour coded, through the machine.

On a four thread overlocker, which is the most common, there are two needle positions. For a more secure seam with a double line of straight stitching, use threads in both needles. When neatening seams and raw edges, use one needle only - the choice of left or right will depend on the desired width of the seam.

Accessories

A rolled hem presser foot is invaluable for stitching tiny hems and seams on lightweight fabrics such as chiffon and organdie. Sometimes a special stitch plate is required as well as the foot. It is easier to work a rolled hem on curved edges using an overlocker.

A blind hem foot and a gathering foot are often available.

An elastic attachment can be a valuable tool, providing a quick way to attach elastic or decorative tapes to a raw edge. The elasticity can be controlled by turning a screw on the attachment.

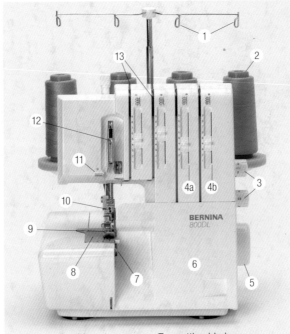

1	thread guides	7	cutting blade - behind cover
2	thread cones	8	stitch plate
3	stitch length regulators	9	presser foot
4a	upper thread looper tension discs	10	needle and housing
4b	lower thread looper tension discs	11	thread guides
5	flywheel	12	take up lever
6	lower looper housing	13	needle thread tension discs

machine needles

Sewing machine needles are available in different sizes, ranging from the finest (size 60) to the most coarse (size 110). Choose a needle that is suited to the type and weight of fabric that you are using and replace it regularly. Discard needles that are bent or burred as they can damage the fabric and are difficult to stitch with. A damaged needle may also result in the machine skipping stitches.

Type	Description	Use	Size	Suitable for
Universal	Standard	General sewing	60, 70 70, 80 80, 90 90, 100	Lightweight natural and synthetic fabric chiffon, georgette, organdie, batiste Artificial silk, linen blends, lingerie fabrics poplin, shirting Ticking, linen, suiting Coating
Jersey/Stretch	Ball point	Knit garments Swimwear	70 75 80, 90 90, 100	Fine jersey, single jersey Jersey, silk jersey Lycra, lingerie fabrics Knits (interlock, rugby)
Jeans	Extra sharp	Outer garments Sportswear	90 - 110	Canvas, cord, denim, heavy twill
Microtex	Extra sharp	Standard clothing	60 - 80	Microfibre, silk
Embroidery	Large eye, highly polished hollow neck, light ball point	Embroidery and specialty threads	75 - 90	Natural or synthetic fabrics
Hemstitch	Wing needle	Embroidery, hemstitching	100	Natural fabrics
Quilting	Light point	Straight and top stitching, decorative stitching	75 - 90	Natural or synthetic fabrics
Leather	Wedge shaped point	Soft leather, vinyl	80, 90 100	Soft leather Leather and vinyl
Metafil	Standard point with large long eye and deep groove	Metallic threads	80	Most natural or synthetic fabrics
Twin Needle	Standard needle double shaft	Tucks, embroidery	70 - 100	Light to medium weight fabric
Triple Needle	Standard needle triple shaft	Tucks, embroidery	80	Light to medium weight fabric

tools

Basic tools such as a good pair of scissors, a selection of pins and needles, tape measure and marking pens are essential to begin sewing. Adding more specialized equipment can be done over time.

Cutting tools

Dressmaking scissors, usually 18cm - 20cm (7" - 8") in length make cutting out the garment easy. Use the full blade when cutting as this ensures a straight cut edge. Buy the best quality you can afford and use for cutting fabric only, as other materials will blunt the blades.

Smaller sewing scissors, 11.5cm - 14cm (4 1/2" - 5 1/2") in length, are useful for trimming and clipping.

Scissors are available with metal, plastic or 'soft grip' handles. Choose scissors that are comfortable to hold. Have scissors professionally sharpened as soon as they show signs of wear. Dead spots along the length or at the tip of the scissor blades are a common sign of wear. Keep them lubricated by occasionally placing a small drop of oil onto the screw. Wipe away any excess before use.

Thread clippers are handy for small trimming tasks while you sew.

Rotary cutters are excellent for cutting bias binding or straight strips of fabric. They are usually used with a special mat underneath. Replace the blade as soon as it shows signs of wear.

A *seam ripper* or 'quick unpick' makes unpicking easy by cutting through the threads of a seam. It can also be used for cutting open buttonholes.

A *cutting table* provides a wonderful surface for laying and cutting out fabric. Most cutting tables are lightweight and can be folded up and stored.

Marking tools

Fabric marking pens are very handy for transferring any temporary pattern or design markings onto fabric. There are several different types available so choose the one that best suits your needs.

Water-soluble markers are chemical based and leave blue marks that can be removed with water. Do not iron before removing the marks as heat can make them permanent.

Fading markers are also chemical based and leave a purple mark. This will fade away quite quickly, depending on the fabric and the pressure used. Do not iron before they fade.

Chalk based pencils are used on dark fabrics. The chalk is enclosed in a wood casing, similar to a pencil. The marks brush away easily. Other forms of chalk markers are *seam markers* and *tailors' chalk.*

Dressmakers' carbon has a coloured waxy surface on one side that is placed facing the fabric under the pattern. Markings are transferred to the fabric with a scribing tool such as a tracing wheel. It is sold in a variety of colours - dark for light coloured fabrics and vice versa. The marks should be transferred to the wrong side only.

Measuring tools

The *tape measure* is any pliable measuring device. Choose a tape that has increments on both sides and is marked in imperial and metric measurements.

Long wooden or *metal rulers* are useful for marking long lines such as cutting lines, frills, bindings and bias strips.

A *sewing guage* has a sliding tab, making it easy to measure pleats, the depth of a hem, the length of a buttonhole and the spaces between them.

A *hem marker* is a useful tool to measure the level of a hem, making it consistent around the skirt.

Pins and needles

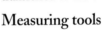

Varying in style, there is a type of pin for every task. A good, all purpose pin is a medium length glass headed pin with a fine shaft. Glass heads will not melt if ironed and are easy to find if dropped on the floor. Silk pins have a longer, finer shaft than regular pins and glide easily through fabrics. They are available with glass or plain heads.

For handsewing, crewel or sharps needles in a selection of sizes is recommended.

Discard any pins or needles that are damaged in any way. Store your needles in their packets or a needle case. Pins should be kept in a moisture proof container with a tight lid, to prevent rust. A small sachet of silica gel in the container will help.

General tools

Some tools and aids have been developed to make specific tasks easier.

A *point turner* makes pushing out tight corners easier.

A *loop turner* is a fine metal rod with a latch on the end which is used to turn rouleau strips to the right side.

Bias binding makers are used to fold the raw edges of binding strips continuously before they are pressed.

Pin cushions and *magnets* help to contain pins and needles in one place.

A *needle threader* is often helpful to thread machine and hand sewing needles.

Thimbles are available in different materials such as plastic, leather and metal. A thimble protects the top of the finger that is used to push the needle through the fabric. Choose a thimble that fits snugly over your finger.

Aids such as anti-fray sprays and liquids, fusible tapes, glues and tacking sprays are available. Before using these products on any fabric, read the manufacturer's instructions carefully.

fabric | care symbols

Common symbols appearing on garment or fabric labels provide care instructions from the manufacturer.

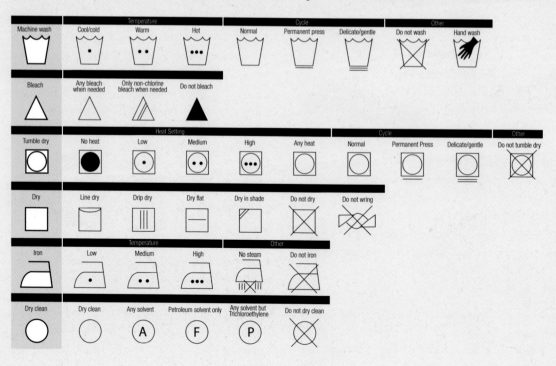

fabric fibres

Care instructions are intended as a guide only. It is advisable to check the manufacturer's instructions before you launder as individual fabrics may have more specific requirements.

Type	Fabric	Features	Care instructions
Cotton	Batiste, broadcloth, broderie anglaise, buckram, calico, chambray, chintz, corduroy, damask, denim, duck, flannelette, gingham, homespun, lace, lawn, muslin, net, organdie, piqué, poplin, sailcloth, sateen, seersucker, terry cloth, ticking, velvet, velveteen, voile, waffle	Cool to wear. Absorbant, porous and accepts dyes easily. Strong fibre but tends to crease easily. Deteriorates with mildew and colour fades in sunlight. Shrinks unless treated, so pre-shrink before use.	Warm to hot machine wash. Can be bleached and tumble dried. Iron while damp.
Wool	Broadcloth, challis, crepé, flannel, gabardine, serge, tweed, worsted	Insulating properties make it warm to wear. Flame and wrinkle resistant. Susceptible to moth damage.	Dry clean. Shrink resistant wools may be machine washed. Steam iron. Use pressing cloth.
Silk	Batiste, broadcloth, brocade, charmeuse, chiffon, crepe de chine, georgette, habutai, lace, organza, shantung, tussah silk, velvet	Soft, lustrous fabrics that drape well. Cool or warm to wear. Deteriorates with mildew and perspiration. Fades in sunlight. Susceptible to moth damage.	Usually dry clean, some may be washed if softness is required. Cool iron on the wrong side.
Linen	Damask, handerchief linen, suiting, many medium to heavy weight fabrics with a textured surface	Strong, absorbent fibre. Draws heat from the body, making it cool to wear. Creases easily and has a tendency to shrink.	Dry clean to keep crisp polished finish.
Synthetic	Acetate, acrylic, lace, lycra, nylon, rayon, satin, taffeta, tulle	Crease resistant. Some have a silk like lustre, drape well and dry quickly. Most collect static electricity. Acrylics have low absorbancy and resist wrinkles, moths and mildew. Have a tendency to pill.	Launder fabrics according to their specific requirements.
Blends	Batiste, broadcloth, brocade, broderie anglaise, chambray, chiffon, chintz, damask, gabardine, gingham, homespun, lawn, muslin, piqué, polycotton, seersucker, voile	Being a blend of two or more fibres, the combination is designed to highlight the best properties of each.	Launder according to the most sensitive fibre in the blend.
Knits (silk, cotton, wool, blended fibres)	Bouclé, double knit, fleece and polar knits, jersey, rib, rugby, stretch towelling, tricot, velour	Strong fibres and construction. High polyester content ensures crease resistance and durability but may have a tendency to pill.	Follow care instructions for the fibre used.
Non-woven	Felt, fur, leather, plastic, suede, vinyl	Materials used for their durability and strength. These features can make them difficult to stitch.	Plastic and vinyl can be wiped clean - all others should be dry cleaned.

fabrics

The infinite variety of fabrics available can be reduced to three main elements - fibre content, method of manufacture and weight. There are two main types of fibre used to make fabric - natural and synthetic. Weaving, knitting and bonding are the processes used to turn yarn into fabric. The weight of the fabric can range from a voile so sheer you can see through it, to the heavy woollen worsted fabrics used for suits and coats.

Fibres

Natural fibres such as cotton, wool, silk and linen have all the subtle irregularities and intrinsic beauty present in nature. They are absorbent and porous, making them very reactive to dyes, temperature and humidity. Cotton and wool especially, are comfortable to wear in very different climatic situations, whereas a garment made from silk, enables the wearer to remain cool on hot days and warm in cold conditions.

Natural fibres may have a limited lifespan and they may be susceptible to insect damage or mildew. However with appropriate care they can be very long lasting.

Linen is one of the world's oldest fibres. It is manufactured from the fibrous stalks of the flax plant and comes in various weights for different purposes. Ramie refers to a fibre from the nettle family of plants, mainly grown in Asia. It is sometimes blended with cotton for less expensive clothing and is often confused with linen. Its care is similar to linen but if blended with other fibres, follow the manufacturer's instructions.

Silk yarn is the longest natural filament used to make fabric. It is produced when the cocoon of the silkworm is

unwound. Wild silk (tussah) is made from the cocoons of silkworms that live in uncultivated conditions, eating a varied diet. It is naturally darker in colour and cannot be bleached.

Synthetic fibres are produced in a laboratory using chemical processes that combine elements such as petroleum products, alcohol, gasses, water or air. This class of fabrics include polyester, nylon, acrylic, lycra, polyurethane and metallic fibres such as Lurex. Rayon was the first synthetic fibre, developed as a more affordable replacement for silk.

Viscose and acetate are also synthetic fibres but they are made from cellulose - a natural product.

Synthetic fabrics are very strong and resilient but lack the absorbancy and temperature transference properties of natural fibres.

Blended fibres are produced by combining natural and synthetic fibres to contain the best attributes of both. Polycotton, a blend of polyester and cotton, is the most widely used blend. It combines the strength and crease resistance of polyester with the comfort and softness of cotton.

Woven, non-woven or knitted

Weaving is the interlacing of yarns, on a machine called a loom. The stronger warp yarns are fixed lengthwise and interwoven at right angles with the often weaker weft yarn.

There are three main weaves - plain, twill and satin. A plain weave is a thread being passed under and over the warp threads in one row, then alternating the passing sequence in the next row.

In a twill weave, the weft thread passes over two or more warp threads in one row and moves one thread to the right or left in each successive row. This forms diagonal ridges on the surface of the fabric.

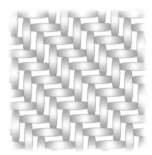

Patterned weaves, such as dobby, damask and Jacquard are complex structures that produce an intricate, textured surface with areas of satin weave pattern against a plain or twill background.

Knit fabrics are based on the age old technique of knitting by hand. Knitting machines produce fabrics with a similar structure with stitches on a much smaller scale. Complicated knit variations can be produced by changing the arrangement of knit and purl stitches. Rows of loops formed along the length of a knit fabric are called ribs. Another feature of knit fabrics is elasticity. This makes them particularly suited to use for casual clothing and sportswear.

Non-woven fabrics are produced with processes such as felting and netting.

Felting is the oldest method of making fabric. Short fibres are matted together using heat, moisture and agitation or pressure, creating a thick, pliable sheet that doesn't fray.

Netting is a twisted or knotted structure that produces an open mesh. Tulle and cotton net are plain styles of netting. To make lace, intricate floral or geometric patterns are woven into the mesh, using finer or coarser threads than those forming the netting.

interfacing

When constructing a garment, interfacing can be applied to the wrong side of the fabric pieces to provide shape and stability.

Interfacings come in light, medium and heavy weights and can be stitched or fused to the fabric. They may be woven or non-woven and consist of natural or synthetic fibres. The colours are limited to white, black, grey and ecru. Choose an interfacing that matches the care requirements and weight of your fabric, remembering that the interfacing should always be the same weight or lighter than the garment fabric and that your pattern may require more than one type. For sheer fabrics where interfacing may show through, another piece of the garment fabric is a good alternative to interfacing.

There are pre-cut interfacings for waistbands, cuffs and button bands. They have seamline and fold markings that make it easier to keep the seams and folds evenly spaced.

Woven interfacings are usually cut on the straight grain, matching the grain of the fabric piece. Non-woven types have no grain and can be cut in any direction.

Stretch non-woven interfacings have a certain amount of crosswise stretch, making them ideal for knit fabrics.

Interfacings are generally attached to facings or linings but lightweight types often work better when applied to the garment pieces. Personal preference can play a large part in determining on what layer the interfacing is placed, bearing in mind that it should never be obvious on the right side of the garment.

notions

Notions are the additional items, besides the fabric and pattern that you'll need to finish your garment.

Buckles and clasps

Stiffened belts, shoulder straps and swimwear pieces are some instances where these types of fastenings are used.

Buckles can be bought as a complete unit or as bare metal or plastic to be covered with fabric.

A *dungaree buckle* comes in two pieces - the clip, which is secured onto the end of the straps through adjuster bars and a metal jean button that is attached to the bib with a rivet.

A *bikini clasp* is used to secure the narrow ends of a bra top at the midriff.

Elastic

Most elastics are made from a rubber core covered in cotton or synthetic thread. They may occur as a single strand, such as shirring and hat elastic, or as several rows braided together. When choosing elastic, look for one with the most suitable features for the style and use of the garment.

Braided elastics can be identified by the lengthwise parallel ridges that give them a stronger grip. This type of elastic narrows when stretched and is recommended for casings rather than stitching to the garment itself.

Woven elastics are usually softer and the edges curl less when stretched than the braided types. This makes them more suitable to stitch directly onto the fabric.

Non-roll elastic is constructed with vertical ribs to keep it from twisting within a casing.

Lace

Lace is available in dress widths or in quite narrow forms used as trimming. Styles range from delicate mesh laces like malines or valenciennes, to more sturdy types such as cluny and guipure. Broderie anglaise, an embroidered eyelet lace, is another widely used trimming.

Lace can also be divided into groups according to the number of decorative or straight edges it has. Edging lace has one decorative side, with the remaining edge being used to attach it to the fabric.

Insertion lace has two finished edges, often decorative. This is either applied to the right side leaving the fabric behind the lace, or is inserted between two pieces of fabric. Beading is a type of insertion lace with a series of decorative holes along the centre, or to one side, for ribbon to be threaded through.

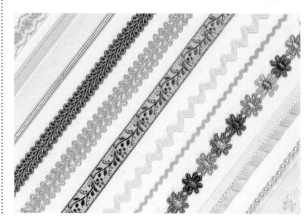

Ribbon, braid and cord

Ribbons are used extensively to decorate garments and homewares. Some forms are satin, velvet, moiré, looped or ruffle edge, grosgrain, petersham and woven Jacquard ribbon with delicate woven designs. They may be stitched flat, threaded through beading, folded into bows, used as ties and sashes or rolled and folded into three dimensional roses and rosebuds - the uses are endless.

Braids are bulkier and have more texture than ribbons. Some of the most common types are silky, Russia and scroll braids. Russia braid is stitched to the fabric along the centre groove. The others are stitched along both sides.

Ricrac has zigzag edges and is often classed as a braid. This can be stitched flat, shaped to follow a curve or stitched into a seam to expose the points on one side.

Twisted cords made from cotton or rayon, are used in drawstring casings or home furnishings. Fine cords are enclosed in fabric to make corded piping and to define twin needle pintucks.

Tapes and binding

Cotton tapes stabilise seams that would otherwise stretch adding structure and firmness. Fusible tapes eliminate the need to tack or secure with stitching.

Petersham tape is used to stiffen waistbands. It has ridges impregnated with rubber to prevent movement.

Belt backing or waistband stiffening is fused to one side of a waistband or slipped through a fabric belt to provide support.

Binding is used to finish a raw edge. It is cut on the bias, allowing it to be shaped to fit a curve. Binding is available in several widths and a myriad of colours. Satin bias binding makes an attractive alternative to plain fabric types.

Boning is made from nylon or plastic and is used to add shape and support to the seams of a bodice, usually in strapless styles. It is threaded through a channel sewn into the seam allowance. Covered boning is simply stitched to the seam allowance along the sides of the tape covering.

Beads, sequins and other trinkets

Embellishing your garments is easy with the many different forms of beads, sequins, jewels and charms available. Designing your decoration and stitching the elements on individually may be time consuming. Ready-made motifs are quickly attached by sewing around the edge by hand or machine.

Fastenings

Zips are available in three main types - conventional, open end and invisible. Conventional and invisible dress zips are divided at one end while open end zips can be separated at both ends.

All zips consist of metal or nylon teeth embedded into fabric tape, or a synthetic coil stitched to fabric tape. Both styles include a metal slider that opens and closes the interlocking teeth of the zip. Metal clips or melted nylon 'stops' are positioned at the upper and lower ends to prevent the slider slipping off.

Buttons are probably the oldest form of closure. Made from bone they were stitched on with dried sinew and pushed through holes in an animal hide. Although times have changed, the button is still one of the most common forms of garment closure.

Buttons are available in an infinite number of styles, sizes, shapes and colours. When choosing one that is right for the garment, keep in mind that a novelty button with sharp or odd angles, may not be a suitable or practical form of closure. They are difficult to pass through a buttonhole and are best used as decoration only.

Fabric covered buttons provide a suitable alternative when the perfect ready-made button cannot be found. If making your own, follow the manufacturer's instructions carefully to obtain the best results.

Hook and loop tape is also known as *Velcro*. The surface of one tape has a fuzzy, looped nap that locks into the hooked nap of the other tape when pressed together. It is available in various widths and a range of colours.

Threads

Sewing thread should be strong, durable and pliable, ensuring it will resist breaking under the strain of passing through the machine under tension. It is important to match the needle size to the thread chosen. If the needle is too small, the thread will fray and break easily. If the needle size is too large, the thread will not fill the needle holes punctured through the fabric.

Thread sizes are expressed as a number - the higher the number, the finer the thread. A medium weight thread suitable for most fabrics is no. 50.

Natural sewing threads include cotton, silk and linen. Cotton and silk are both suitable for machine sewing. Linen and strong cotton threads, wrapped around a polyester core, are

usually confined to hand sewing tasks that require extra thread strength.

Synthetic threads are made from spun polyester or sometimes nylon. There are also polyester and cotton blends, which are strong all-purpose threads.

All threads have a silicone or polished finish which allows it to pass through the machine and the fabric with ease.

Choose a thread slightly darker than the background colour for plain fabrics. For prints, spots or checks, the thread colour should match the dominant fabric colour.

General purpose threads have a spun polyester core wrapped in cotton. It is stronger and has more elasticity than other threads and is suitable for all fabrics. This thread comes in the widest range of colours and sizes.

Pure cotton threads are used for a wide variety of tasks, from fine heirloom sewing to quilting and topstitching by hand or machine. They are usually finished with a process called mercerizing which gives a lustrous sheen. Cotton threads do not have much give and are therefore not recommended for use with knit fabrics.

Silk is a fine, strong sewing thread with a soft, pearly sheen. It is used for silk lingerie, heirloom baby gowns and some fine woollen fabrics.

Metallic thread usually has a cotton or polyester core, loosely wrapped with a gold, silver or copper metallic fibre. It is commonly used for embroidery by hand or machine. Treat it carefully when pressing, as these threads do not respond well to heat or steam.

Invisible thread made from nylon, is a strong, transparent monofilament thread that comes in two shades - light and dark. It is commonly used for hems and can be useful when you are unable to find a thread shade to match your fabric.

body measurements

Accurate measurements are essential for choosing the appropriate pattern size and for making any adjustments to obtain the best fit. Have a friend help you with these.

Take the measurements in bare feet, wearing only under garments or figure hugging clothing. Tie a ribbon around your waist and adjust it to your natural waistline.

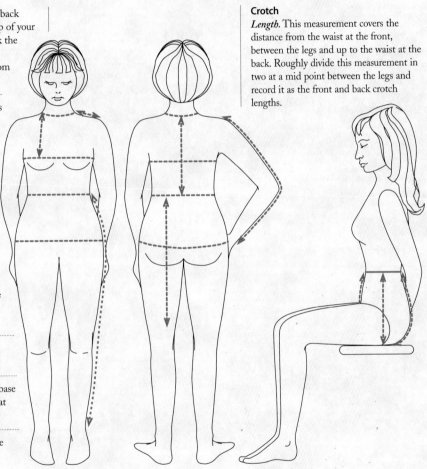

Height. Stand straight with your back against a wall. Place a ruler on top of your head and at 90° to the wall. Mark the wall at the end of the ruler. Step away and measure your height from the floor to the mark.

Bust. (On children or men, this is the chest measurement). Place the tape measure around your chest with the tape across the fullest part of the bust and the widest section of the back.

Bust point. Take a measurement between the high point of the shoulder to the tip of the breast.

Waist. Measure around the waist at the position of the ribbon. Leave the ribbon in place as a marker for other measurements.

Hips. Measure around the fullest part of the hips and bottom.

Back length. Measure from the base of the neck, to the waist marker at the back.

Shoulder. Place the tape measure from the natural neckline to the edge of the shoulder joint.

Sleeve length. With your hand on your hip, measure from the shoulder joint, over the elbow and down to the wrist.

Trouser length. Measure down the side of one leg from the waist marker to the ankle joint, or the preferred trouser length.

Skirt length. Measure from the waist marker at the back, over the fullness of the bottom and down to the preferred length for the style of skirt.

Neck. Place the tape measure around your neck at the lowest position where it joins into the shoulder line.

Crotch

Length. This measurement covers the distance from the waist at the front, between the legs and up to the waist at the back. Roughly divide this measurement in two at a mid point between the legs and record it as the front and back crotch lengths.

Depth. Sitting on a solid flat chair, straighten your back and measure between the waist marker and the seat of the chair at your side.

15

patterns

A pattern is a set of templates provided so that a copy can be made of an original model. A sewing pattern contains not only the pattern pieces but also additional information.

Pattern cover

Photographs or drawings on the pattern envelope show the style and form of the original garment or object. The front and back view drawings will give an indication of the complexity of the project. Besides the main garment design, patterns usually have alternative styling options.

On the back, charts display standard body measurements in metric and imperial units, as well as finished garment measurements and the fabric, linings, interfacing and notions required for each size. There are also suggestions for suitable fabrics to use.

Size

Patterns are drafted from a set of standard body measurements based on the average sizes of the population. Refer to page 15 for taking measurements.

Your pattern size may be the same as, or close to, your ready-to-wear size, however a sewing pattern size should be directly related to your measurements.

The actual measurements of a pattern will not exactly match yours. Except for garments made from stretch fabrics, a garment should have room for the wearer to stretch, bend, reach and walk. This is called wearing ease and is already incorporated into the pattern. Patterns designed specifically for knit fabrics include less wearing ease because the fabric stretches. Woven fabrics should not be substituted in patterns for stretch knits as there will not be enough wearing ease to make the garment comfortable.

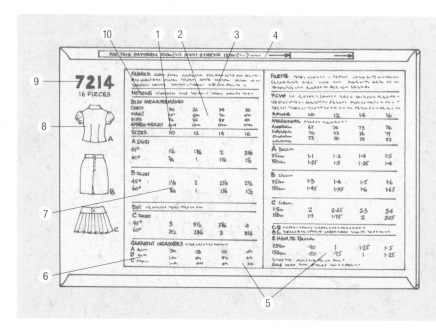

The pattern envelope back

1. sizes included
2. standard body measurements
3. suggested fabrics
4. stretch indicator if applicable
5. pattern statistics, measurements and conversions
6. finished garment measurements
7. fabric requirements for each view
8. back view illustrations
9. pattern catalogue number
10. notions required

Specific body measurements will determine the pattern size for different garment types. As the fit is closer on the upper body, the size of a woman's dress, coat, shirt or jacket pattern is chosen by the bust measurement. For men and children, this is the chest measurement. Use this as the primary measurement. Trousers and skirt sizes are chosen by the hip measurement and should be the main consideration when a pattern contains both upper and lower garments. If any measurement falls between the standard measurements, choose the larger size.

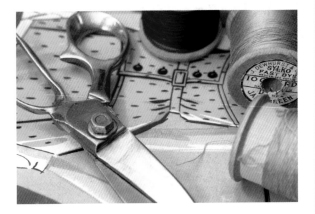

Multi-sized patterns

These patterns have the cutting lines for several sizes printed on the same pattern piece. Each size has a line with a different arrangement of dashes or dots.
A solid line usually denotes a line common to all sizes.

Trace the lines and markings for the desired size onto lightweight interfacing or tracing paper. Tracing the pieces keeps the original intact and tracings are more durable than tissue paper patterns. You can also make slight adjustments between the lines to take your own measurements into account. For instance, your waistline might be the same as one of the smaller sizes but your hips match a larger one. Draw a line between the two on your tracing.

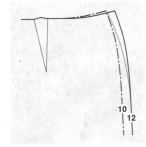

Symbols

Pattern pieces are defined by a series of lines, arrows, dots and symbols common to all pattern brands. The pattern symbols are usually explained in a chart. Solid or dashed outer lines, marked with a size, are the cutting lines. Seam allowances are marked with a particular measurement or a line of long dashes.

Every pattern piece should have a line with arrows at both ends, denoting the direction of the fabric grain. It is important to pin the pattern piece to the fabric aligning the grainline.

Pairs of adjustment lines are printed at the best positions to make alterations to the length of a pattern piece. If there is more than one set of double lines, it is best to divide the adjustment between the positions rather than make it in one.

Triangular notches are usually points to align when matching the raw edges of two garment pieces. Bent arrows show that an edge should be placed on the fold when cutting out. Other markings may include zip, buttonhole, button, pleat, dart and interfacing placement symbols. Most symbols should be transferred to the wrong side of the fabric after cutting out.

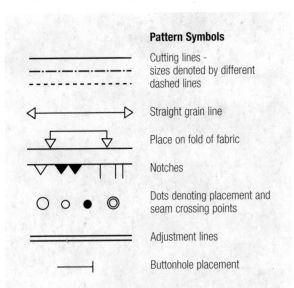

Pattern Symbols

Symbol	Description
	Cutting lines - sizes denoted by different dashed lines
	Straight grain line
	Place on fold of fabric
	Notches
	Dots denoting placement and seam crossing points
	Adjustment lines
	Buttonhole placement

patterns

Altering patterns

When making adjustments to any pattern pieces always stitch a trial or toile using an inexpensive fabric first. Further alterations may be necessary before cutting into your final fabric. Any changes should be made to all corresponding pattern pieces.

Lengthening

Cut through the pattern piece between the adjustment lines. Centre a piece of tracing paper under the separation point. Spread the two pattern pieces for the required distance. Keep the 'place on fold' line matching if the piece has one, otherwise centre the lower piece under the upper piece. Check the distance with a ruler and tape or pin the pattern pieces to the paper. Continue any pattern lines on the paper (diag 1). Trim away any excess paper.

For a skirt, tape or pin a piece of paper at the lower edge of the pattern piece. Using a ruler, measure and mark dots for the new hemline at approximately 5cm (2") intervals below the curve. Join the dots and then rule a line to extend the sides (diag 2).

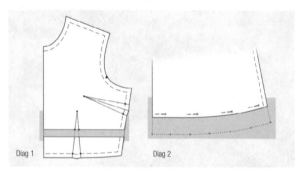

Diag 1   Diag 2

Shortening

Measure and rule a line below the uppermost adjustment line at the required distance. Fold the pattern piece on the adjustment line and bring the fold down to meet the new line. Tape or pin in place, ensuring any 'place on fold' lines are straight. If the sides are uneven, redraw the lines to meet on the upper and lower edges of the pleat formed in the pattern piece (diag 3).

For a skirt, measure and mark dots for the new hemline at approximately 5cm (2") intervals above the curve. Join the dots and trim off the excess (diag 4).

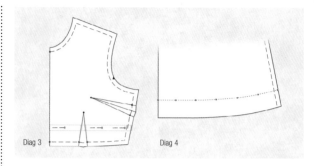

Diag 3   Diag 4

Adjusting the shoulder width

To prepare a pattern piece for a shoulder alteration, rule a line from the centre of the shoulder, roughly parallel to the armhole. Rule another line to the armhole notch. Shoulder adjustments should be done on both the front and back bodice pieces.

1. Increasing the width of the shoulder. Cut through the marked lines. Keeping the armhole points touching, spread the armhole and shoulder corner until the shoulder line matches your measurement. Tape a piece of paper behind and secure. Redraw the shoulder line between the outer points (diag 5).

2. Decreasing the shoulder width. Cut through the marked lines. Rotate the shoulder corner inwards, overlapping the pieces until the shoulder line matches your measurement. Tape together and redraw the shoulder line between the outer points (diag 6).

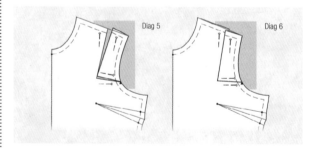

Diag 5   Diag 6

Bust dart

A small adjustment to the height of a bust dart may be achieved by simply raising or lowering the bust point. For large adjustments, the entire dart should be raised or lowered to ensure the correct fit. Measure 2.5cm (1") from the point of the bust dart and compare your measurement to this point (diag 7).

1. Lowering the bust dart. Cut horizontally across the pattern above the dart and vertically down past the dart point. Pleat the pattern below the dart for the depth required to lower the bust point. Tape a piece of paper behind and secure. Redraw the side edge between the armhole and the dart. Lower the point of the waist dart by the same measurement (diag 8).

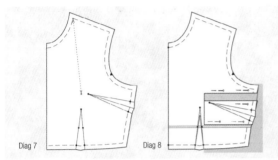

Diag 7   Diag 8

2. Raising the bust dart. Cut across the pattern below the dart and vertically up past the dart point. Pleat the pattern above the dart for the depth required to raise the bust point. Tape a piece of paper behind and secure. Redraw the side edge. Increase the point of the waist dart by the same measurement (diag 9).

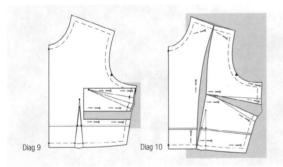

Diag 9   Diag 10

3. Increasing the bust fullness. Cut vertically from the inside edge of the waist dart to the centre of the shoulder. Cut horizontally from the centre front to the bust point and along the centre of the dart. Place paper behind and spread the pieces apart. Keep the shoulder and lower edge points touching on the vertical line.

Example: To increase the bust measurement from 95cm (37 3/8") to 105cm (41 3/8") spread the pieces sideways by 5cm (2"). Increase the length to match your bust point measurement. Tape the pieces in place and redraw the dart (diag 10).

Crotch

Changing the hip and waist measurements alone will not entirely allow for a large tummy or a flat bottom. The crotch length and depth should also be adjusted to ensure the correct fit.

1. Increasing the waist or hip. Make changes in small increments at the side seams (diag 11). Larger adjustments should be distributed between the side seams, darts and the crotch seam on both the front and back pieces.

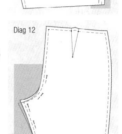

Diag 11

2. Adjusting the length at the crotch point. The following alteration is the easiest way to lengthen the crotch but it also changes the width at the top of the legs. Mark a new crotch point inside or outside the cutting line and redraw the line, tapering to join with the original line (diag 12).

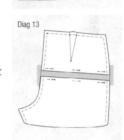

Diag 12

3. Adjusting the depth. Spread out or pleat the pattern at the adjustment line for the required distance on both the front and back pieces (diag 13).

Diag 13

4. Increasing the length at the seam. Cut through the adjustment line. Spread the crotch seam only for the required distance. Tape a piece of paper behind and redraw the crotch line (diag 14).

5. Decreasing the length at the seam. Pleat the adjustment line for the required distance at the crotch seam only, tapering the fold to the side seam. Redraw the crotch line to straighten (diag 15).

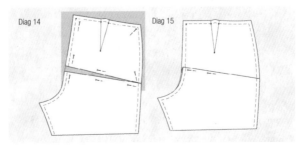

Diag 14   Diag 15

preparation | cutting out

Fabric preparation is essential before you start cutting out. If the fabric has been folded on a bolt, check to see if the foldline can be pressed out when required and to ensure it is not faded.

Hold the fabric up to the light to see if there are any holes or flaws that should be avoided. If you find any, mark them and place them uppermost when you lay the fabric out to ensure they are avoided when pinning the pattern pieces.

Pre-shrink fabrics containing fibres with a tendency to shrink. Refer to the fabric chart on page 9. To prepare the fabric, pre-shrink by laundering following the manufacturer's care instructions.

Grain

When choosing woven fabric be aware that its characteristics may affect garment construction.

The grain of a fabric is indicated by the direction of the yarns, the warp is lengthwise and the weft, crosswise. Any diagonal dissection of the warp and the weft is the bias. The true bias is the 45° angle between them.

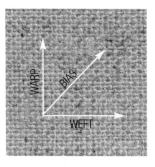

The way a garment hangs or drapes is affected by the grain on which it is cut. Lengthwise grain is the strongest and has very little give or stretch. In most garments this hangs vertically, taking the weight of the garment from shoulder to hem. Crosswise grain is more pliable and drapes differently, giving the garment a softer appearance. Bias grain has the most stretch, allowing it to drape softly. A bias cut dress or skirt should be hung and left until the sections with the greatest stretch have dropped to their lowest level, before the hem is straightened and secured.

The selvedge is the firmly woven strip that forms along each lengthwise edge of the finished fabric. Very few pieces of fabric have both selvedges and grainlines perfectly aligned and at right angles to each other. To achieve the correct alignment, cut the upper and lower edges following a thread in the weave, either by sight or by pulling a thread and cutting along the channel that appears.

Straightening the grain

Fold the fabric in half along the length, matching the selvedges and the upper cut edge. Hold up the length and check if the selvedges stay aligned, or if they fall away from each other.

If they remain aligned or there is very little difference over the entire length of the fabric, proceed to lay it out and cut out the garment pieces.

A greater difference in the way the selvedges hang may be corrected by pressing. If it is really skewed, you may need to review the suitability of the fabric.

Fabric may also be tugged sharply on the bias to bring the yarns back into alignment. Move from the upper corner with the most distortion to the opposite lower corner. This process is best done with two people.

Printed stripes and checks with an obvious off-grain print will make the fabric look crooked even if the grainlines are aligned. Since it is part of the fabric, this cannot be corrected. Check the print in the store and avoid buying fabric with this type of flaw.

Surface direction

Textured fabrics like velvet and velveteens have a napped surface or pile, which changes appearance when placed in the opposite direction. If the pile faces downwards, the colour appears lighter and the surface has a delicate sheen. In the opposite direction, the colour is rich and dense with no sheen at all. Choose the direction you like the best and mark with an arrow on the selvedges. Remember to place each pattern piece in this direction on the layout.

Fabric direction should also be decided for fabrics with a 'shot' weave and for some satins. Check satin fabric by placing two swatches side by side in opposite directions in daylight. If the colour remains the same then it may be possible to rotate pattern pieces on the layout. The same applies for shot fabrics. Choose the colour you like best and lay all the pieces in this direction. The play of light will change the colours with movement, having the same direction will mean the changes are consistent.

Right and wrong side

The right side is usually obvious, however at times you may need to study the fabric carefully to determine the right and wrong sides.

The right side of the fabric has generally been finished to resist marks and pilling. There is no rule to say you can't use the wrong side as the right if you prefer. When there is no apparent difference between the right and wrong sides, choose one and mark this side on all the pieces.

Smooth fabrics usually have a delicate sheen on the right side and appear dull on the wrong. Intricate weaves like Jacquards and dobby cottons are smoother on the right side with loose loops of carried thread on the wrong side. Printed designs are sharper and brighter on the right side and less distinct on the wrong side.

Pattern pieces

Identify all the pattern pieces needed for the chosen view of the garment. Consider any style changes you may wish to make, such as eliminating, trimming or repositioning pockets.

Cut the pattern pieces from the sheets or trace them onto interfacing or tracing paper to preserve the original. This is useful when making alterations, as the altered pattern will only fit the intended wearer. Return all the unused pieces to the envelope to avoid confusion later on. Carefully press out any creases from the pattern pieces with a lukewarm dry iron.

Alter the pattern if necessary, ensuring that the alterations are visible on both sides and that the same alterations have been done on all the corresponding pieces. The length should be checked and altered if necessary before cutting out.

Cutting layouts

The fabric layouts are an import feature of the pattern. They are usually found on the instruction sheet, along with a numbered list of the pattern pieces to identify them on the layouts. Find the layouts for the chosen view and the width of the fabric you are using.

Fabrics with a napped surface should be cut out following a 'with nap' layout. If there is no layout for your fabric width or if you are changing any design details, you may need to do a trial layout based on the nearest fabric width to the one you are using.

Work on the longest surface available. It should be long enough to accommodate the full length of the fabric if possible. It is advisable not to disturb the layout until you have cut out all the pieces.

Determine how the fabric should be folded from the layout. To avoid a permanent mark along the centre of the fabric, double lengthwise folds may be used. Selvedges and design features such as stripes, checks and printed or woven patterns, should align exactly. For slippery or sheer fabrics that shift easily, pin the selvedges together at short intervals.

When positioning the pattern piece take note of the pattern placement direction if you have one marked.

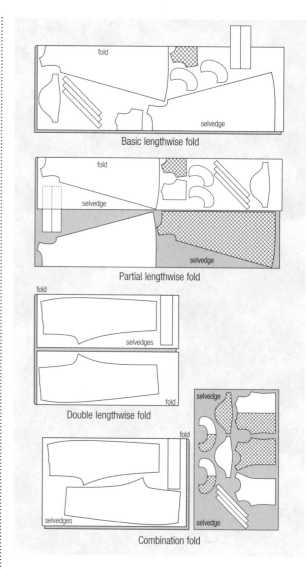

Basic lengthwise fold

Partial lengthwise fold

Double lengthwise fold

Combination fold

hints cutting layouts

Placing matching pieces in opposite directions should only occur on fabrics with no obvious direction.

Shaded or part shaded pattern pieces should be placed with the writing face down for that area.

Pieces extending or with dashed lines should be placed on a single layer of fabric after all others are cut.

Diagonal pieces should be placed on the bias grain.

marking

Transferring markings from the pattern to your cut pieces is important to ensure the best results.

Centre front, back and matched pivot or clipping marks are the most crucial pattern symbols. Other markings may not require transferring.

There are a variety of tools and techniques used in transferring pattern markings onto fabric. Choose a marking method according to the fabric you are using. For example, a mark that can only be removed by dampening the fabric, such as a water-soluble or dissolving pen is unsuitable for dry clean only fabric. Tools that make holes, such as a serrated tracing wheel, are not advisable to use on fabric such as leather because the holes will be permanent. In most cases a combination of marking techniques work best. Always test your marking method on a mall piece of the actual project fabric. The mark should come off easily without damage.

The garment pieces should be marked after you have cut them out. Keep the pattern pieces in place before moving them from the cutting table. Mark most pattern details on the wrong side of the fabric. The few exceptions are the placement markings for surface details such as pockets. Mark both fabric layers unless the marking is intended for one side only, such as a single pocket on a shirt. Buttonholes are marked on one side of the opening and button placements on the corresponding side.

Notching

Cutting notches, V-shaped cuts in the seam allowances to indicate centres, front and back armholes or necklines and the ends of stitchlines, can be a timesaver. Use a pair of scissors that are sharp all the way to the tips.

Fold the fabric at a right angle to the stitchline and snip a small notch out of the seam allowance, ending with the point 4mm ($^3/_{16}$") from the stitchline. This method is not suitable for patterns with narrow seam allowances - 6mm ($^1/_4$") or less.

Tacking

Thread marking takes the most time but is invaluable for fabrics unsuitable for other forms of marking. Lines of tacking can be used to mark the centre front or back lines, fold lines, or the roll line of a collar.

Use contrasting thread. Different colour threads can also be used to distinguish various details. Try to avoid tacking along stitchlines as it may get caught in the stitching.

When the position of a design detail, such as a pocket is required on the right side, trace the position on the wrong side using another marking method, then tack along the marked line to make the marks visible on the front.

Tailors' tacks

Isolated points are best marked with a tailor's tack. They are particularly useful to mark the tip and the matching points along the length of a dart. These thread tacks are worked through a tissue paper pattern piece and two layers of fabric beneath, thereby marking both halves of a garment piece.

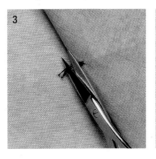

1. Use doubled thread without knotting the end. Take a tiny stitch through the mark on the pattern. Pull the thread through, leaving a 3cm (1$^1/_4$") tail.

2. Take another stitch through the same point and pull through, leaving a 3cm (1$^1/_4$") loop.

3. Trim the thread leaving a 3cm (1$^1/_4$") tail. Carefully pull the pattern piece away. Lift the top layer of fabric to the limit of the thread loops. Snip through the threads midway between the layers of fabric.

4. Open out the garment piece.

marking

pressing

Pressing is an essential part of good garment construction. Have the ironing board with the iron on a low setting ready near your sewing area.

Pressing tools

Irons can vary from a simple model to a deluxe ironing system that includes a large water reservoir and suction board. Common problems with irons are scale buildup in the water tank and a soiled soleplate. Using distilled water or buying an iron with a filter can help to alleviate the scale problem. Cleaning the iron regularly will keep the soleplate in good order.

Ironing boards should be sturdy with a smooth padded cover. Keep the cover clean to prevent marks transferring to the fabric that is being pressed.

Sleeve boards are smaller versions of an ironing board. It enables you to press tight narrow sections of garments such as sleeves.

Pressing hams are very firmly filled pillows of fabric, usually wool on one side and cotton on the other. A pressing ham is used for pressing small areas that are difficult to reach on a flat surface, and for pressing curves and rolling collars.

A *sleeve roll* is cylindrical in shape and similar to a pressing ham. It is particularly useful for pressing sleeves and other parts of a garment that cannot be laid flat.

A *pressing mitt* is a glove shaped device. The mitt is worn on the hand and pushed into areas that cannot be laid flat.

Pressing cloths, also known as rajah cloths, are used when steam ironing and are excellent for setting pleats and removing creases. Pieces of cotton fabric are useful for pressing delicate fabrics, fusing interfacing and appliqué.

Flannelette or fine towelling cloths are helpful when pressing embroidery. Fold the cloth into a pad, place beneath the embroidery and press the back of the fabric.

Pin boards are invaluable when using fabric with a nap such as corduroy or velvet. They resemble a miniature bed of nails. The fabric is laid face down onto the board and pressed from the back. The pins prevent the nap from being pressed flat.

How to press

Pressing is not the same as ironing. When ironing, you move the iron over the fabric to remove creases. Pressing involves very little movement of the iron and more pressure in certain areas. Use a press and lift action rather than gliding over the fabric. Move the iron in the general direction of the straight grain wherever possible.

Pattern instructions will tell you when to press, but as a general rule, press each seam or section before it is crossed by another.

Press on the wrong side or use a pressing cloth to protect the right side from iron shine.

When attaching two different coloured fabrics, the seam should always be pressed towards the darker of the two wherever possible. The dark fabric will conceal the seam on the right side. If this is not possible, grade the darker seam allowance so it is more narrow than the lighter one.

If several seams meet at the same point, aim to press them all open rather than to one side. This will reduce bulk on the wrong side at the junction.

troubleshooting

Type	Problem	Solution
Machine	Machine working but the flywheel isn't turning	• The bobbin case and hook area may be jammed with lint or thread. Pull the bobbin and case out of the hook assembly bed and rock the flywheel back and forth gently while pulling on the thread. Clean out any crevices, using the accessory brush.
	Needle doesn't move	• The needle may still be disengaged from the last time you wound a bobbin. • If the needle is engaged, the flywheel belt may be slipping because its loose or worn.
	Machine and needle working but the fabric isn't feeding through	• Check the presser foot is down and the foot is clamped tight. • The stitch length regulator may be set at 0. • The pressure regulator may be at 0 or in the freeform position. • The feed dogs may be lowered.
Stitching	Stitch length is uneven	• Pulling or pushing the fabric through will cause this. • Pressure regulator might be set too heavy or too light for the fabric.
	Loops are forming on the right or wrong side	• The top thread is incorrectly threaded and tensioned causes loops to form on the wrong side. • Loops on the right side might mean that the bobbin is unevenly wound, incorrectly threaded or not seated in the bobbin case correctly.
	Skipping stitches	• Problems with the needle are the most common cause. It may be blunt or bent, inserted incorrectly or the housing not clamped tight enough. • The needle may be the wrong type for the fabric. • There may be insufficient pressure on the foot.
	Wide stitches pulling in the fabric	• The tension is too tight. • Less tension is needed for zigzag and embroidery stitches. • The fabric may be too sheer - stabilise with spray starch or place interfacing underneath.
Tension	Adjustments don't last	• Tension discs may have worn loose over time - they are replaceable. • Reduce wear on the discs by not pulling the thread through while the presser foot is raised.
Fabric	Layers feed unevenly	• Pressure regulator is too light or too heavy. Stitch more slowly and increase the tension on the upper layer with your hands as you feed the fabric through. Stabilise lightweight or slippery fabrics with spray starch to increase the surface tension or use tearaway stabiliser on top of, or under the fabric, when stitching.
	Stitching puckers the fabric	• The needle and thread may be unsuitable for the fabric. • The stitch tension may be unbalanced. • Stitching will usually pucker a single layer of fabric, unless it has been stabilised.
Thread	Tangling underneath at the beginning of a seam	This can be prevented by placing the needle into the fabric before beginning to stitch. Hold both threads at the back until a few stitches have been formed, then let go.
	Thread and fabric has been pushed into the stitch plate hole.	Rock the flywheel backwards and forwards while pulling on the fabric to release the tangle. Snip the threads and pull out any loose ends. Start the stitching again.

appliqué

This is a French term meaning 'to apply'. The simplest form of appliqué is worked by stitching cut fabric shapes to a base fabric, forming a design or pattern.

A design with simple shapes works best. Details can be added using embroidery or embellishment such as beads or buttons, after the basic shapes have been attached.

Almost any fabric is suitable for appliqué but as a general rule, choose smooth densely woven fabric for the background and lightweight fabrics with similar laundering properties for the design shapes. Appliqué may be stitched by machine or by hand, depending on the effect you wish to achieve.

Fused and handstitched appliqué

before you start

1. Launder the fabrics to remove the sizing and any chemical residue. This will ensure the fabrics bond properly.

2. If the base fabric is lightweight or stretchy, it should be stabilised with interfacing to provide a firm base for stitching.

3. Appliqué by hand or machine may be done in a hoop. This will ensure that the base fabric does not become puckered or distorted.

4. When piecing, aim to match the grain of the appliqué pieces with that of the base fabric wherever possible.

hints
hand appliqué

While machine stitching secures the raw edges of the pieced fabric, hand stitching is not as dense. Therefore it may be necessary to allow for turnings on the pieces to hide the raw edges.

Fusible webbing makes the pieced fabric less likely to fray, so turnings are not always crucial.

preparation for fused appliqué

Modern fusible appliqué papers used to bond fabric pieces have made the preparation and stitching of appliqué much easier than more traditional methods. The shapes are traced onto the smooth side of the paper as a mirror image to ensure correct orientation when attached to the base fabric. The internal design lines defining each element will be stitched as if they are separate pieces of fabric.

Read the manufacturer's instructions carefully before you start using fusible products and ensure the fabrics you choose are compatible with the heat setting required for the product.

Choose a design and simplify the shapes within it if necessary. Consider the colours you wish to use and collect pieces of fabric to suit.

1. Trace the design using a permanent pen. Tape over a light source. Place the base fabric over the design, right side up. Using a sharp lead pencil, trace the design outline only, onto the fabric.

2. Reposition the tracing over the light source with the reverse side up. Place appliqué paper over the tracing with the smooth side up. Trace the individual elements, grouped according to the fabrics used.

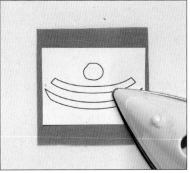

3. Place each piece with the rough side down on the appropriate fabric. Position the iron firmly in the centre of the paper for a few seconds before moving it around to fuse the piece.

4. Allow to cool. Cut out the elements, leaving a small seam allowance on any edges that will be covered by an adjacent shape.

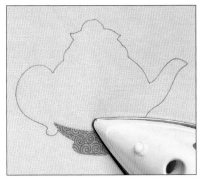

5. Remove the paper backing. Begin with the elements layered beneath adjacent areas. Position and fuse in place right side up.

6. Continue to build the design, layering the elements to secure the raw edges. Draw the internal design lines using a fabric marker.

appliqué

machine appliqué

It is essential to use an open-toed embroidery presser foot on the machine. This has a groove underneath that glides easily over the ridge of decorative stitching and the open front enables you to see where you are sewing. Work with a very close zigzag stitch in a width appropriate to the scale of the design. The stitch length is usually just above 0 to produce a good satin stitch.

1. Position the work under the presser foot with the needle slightly to the right of the edge. Stitch along the edge, allowing the needle to enter the shape on the left and just clear it on the right.

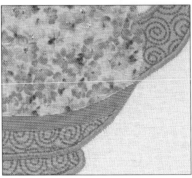

2. Stitching order. Stitch around each element, starting and finishing so the ends will be covered by subsequent stitching.

3. Stitch the edges of the remaining elements in the same manner. Press carefully on the wrong side.

turning corners and curves

1. Outside corners. Stitch to the corner point, stopping with the needle down on the right hand side. Lift the presser foot. Pivot the fabric so that the next edge is ready to stitch.

2. Inside corners. Stitch into the corner the same distance as the stitch width. Stop with the needle down on the left hand side. Lift the presser foot. Pivot the fabric and continue as before.

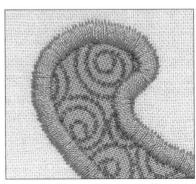

3. Curves. Stop with the needle down on the outside of the curve. Lift the presser foot and slightly rotate the fabric into the curve, then continue. The tighter the curve, the more frequently you will need to stop.

armholes

armhole – bound

This is a method for neatening the raw edge of the armhole on a sleeveless garment. The binding may be made from the same fabric or a contrast fabric. As the armhole is curved, the binding should be cut on the true bias, following the instructions on page 36.

single binding

Preparation. Stitch, neaten and press the shoulder and side seams of the bodice. Determine the desired finished width of the binding. Cut a bias strip to fit around each armhole, cutting it four times the finished width and adding twice the width of the binding to the length. The binding will be attached using the same seam allowance as the finished width.

Example. For a 1cm ($^3/_8$") wide finished binding, cut the bias strip 4cm (1 $^1/_2$") wide and 4cm (1 $^1/_2$") longer than the armhole measurement.

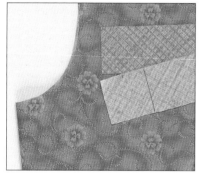

1. Mark a square the same width as the binding on the wrong side of the left hand end. Mark the upper raw edge in the centre of the square.

2. Press under the seam allowance on the lower raw edge of the binding. With right sides together and the centre mark aligned with the side seam, pin the binding around the armhole.

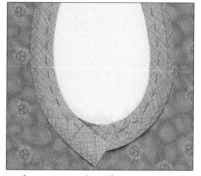

3. As you near the sideseam, mark the upper edge of the binding to match the previous mark. Rule a square with the mark at the centre. Trim any excess binding if required.

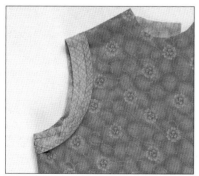

4. Remove a few pins and join the ends of the binding following steps 3 and 4 on page 38. Re-pin and tack the binding in place. Stitch around the armhole.

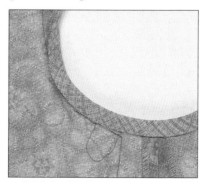

5. Fold the binding to the wrong side and handstitch in place to the previous stitch line.

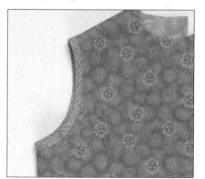

6. Press the binding carefully.

double binding

In this method, the binding is used as a double layer, providing a firmer bound edge.

Preparation

Stitch, neaten and press the shoulder and side seams of the bodice. Determine the desired finished width of the binding. Cut a bias strip to fit around each armhole, cutting it six times the finished width and adding the width of the binding to the length. The binding will be attached using the same seam allowance as the finished width.

Example

For a 1cm ($^3/_8$") wide finished binding, cut the bias strip 6cm (2 $^3/_8$") wide and 6cm (2 $^3/_8$") longer than the armhole measurement.

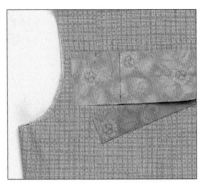

1. Fold the binding in half along the length and press. Open out the right hand end. Mark a square the same width as the binding on the wrong side.

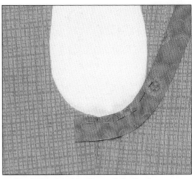

2. Refold the binding. Mark the upper raw edge in the centre of the square. Aligning the mark with the side seam and matching raw edges, begin to pin the binding around the armhole.

3. Remove pins from either side of the side seam. Join the ends of the binding following steps 3 and 4 on page 38. Trim the seam and press open.

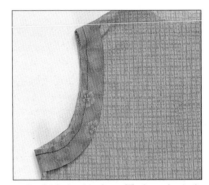

4. Refold the binding. Tack and stitch around the armhole.

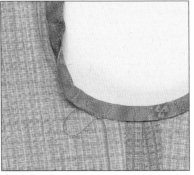

5. Fold the binding to the wrong side and handstitch in place to the previous stitchline.

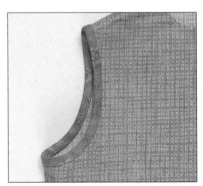

6. Press the binding carefully.

armhole - faced

Preparation

Cut the facings using the appropriate pattern pieces or draft your own referring to the instructions on page 98. If any adjustments are made to the armhole edge, ensure you alter the facing piece too. Apply interfacing to the wrong side of the facing pieces.

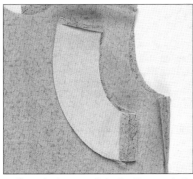

1. Staystitch around the bodice armhole edges. Stitch, neaten and press the shoulder and side seams. Join the facing pieces. Trim the seam allowances and press open. Neaten the outer edge of the facing.

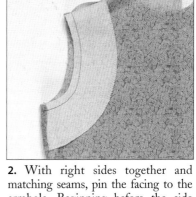

2. With right sides together and matching seams, pin the facing to the armhole. Beginning before the side seam, stitch around the armhole, then overstitch the seam for a short distance.

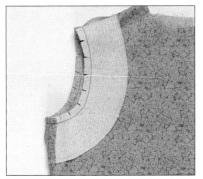

3. Clip the seam allowance and trim to 6mm ($^1/_4$").

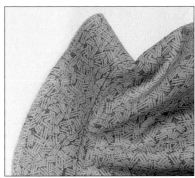

4. Press the facing away from the bodice. Understitch around the armhole on the facing.

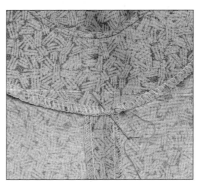

5. Fold the facing to the inside and press. Matching seams, handstitch the facing to the shoulder and side seams, stitching through the bodice seam allowance only.

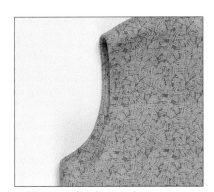

6. Press the faced armhole.

hint altering armholes for binding

If using a pattern not specifically designed for bound armholes, cut away the seam allowance on the armhole edge.

Note that the armhole may be designed for a set-in sleeve that makes it a little deeper than necessary, or the shoulder line might extend further than the top of the arm. Trimming away less at the underarm and more at the shoulder should result in a better finish.

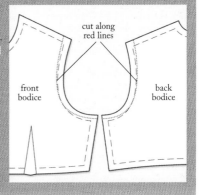

cut along red lines

front bodice

back bodice

belts

Belts can take a multitude of forms and although they can be viewed as a decorative fashion element, they are also practical. Except for soft tie belts, most belts need some form of reinforcing. Shaped belts should be made with a heavier weight interfacing such as buckram. For straight belts, the fabric is stretched taut around a special strip of belt stiffening to give a firm finish.

tie belt

Preparation. Cut a piece of fabric long enough to fit comfortably around the body at the desired position, adding extra length for the knot and ties. Cut twice the desired width, plus seam allowances on both long edges. Mark the centre of the long edges.

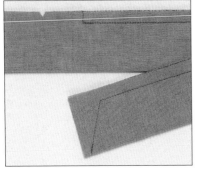  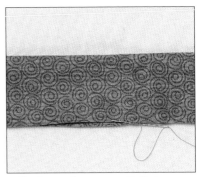

1. Fold the fabric right sides together, matching raw edges and pin. Beginning 2.5cm (1") from the centre mark, stitch along the raw edge. Pivot at the corner, stitch across the end and secure.

2. Return to the centre and stitch the remaining half in the same manner. Clip the corners and turn the belt to the right side through the opening.

3. Push out the corners. Roll the seam to the edge and press, pressing the folded seam allowances across the opening. Handstitch the opening closed using ladder stitch. Press.

straight belt

The instructions on the following page show a self-covered buckle, but any buckle the same width as the belt stiffening may be used. If the buckle has no prong, wrap the raw end of the belt around the bar in the middle and secure in the same manner as step 7. Eyelets are not required for this type of buckle but the keeper should be added.

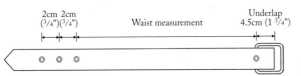

2cm 2cm (¾")(¾")   Waist measurement   Underlap 4.5cm (1 ¾")

Preparation Adding 20cm (8"), cut a strip of belt stiffening to fit comfortably around the waist. Trim one end to a shallow point. Cut the fabric 2cm (³/₄") longer and twice the width, adding a 1cm (³/₈") seam allowance on each long edge. Adding 2cm (³/₄") to the length, make a keeper to fit around the belt, following steps 1 and 2 on page 34.

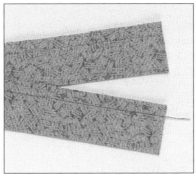

1. With right sides together, fold the fabric in half along the length and pin. Stitch the long edge using a 1cm (³/₈") seam allowance.

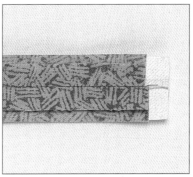

2. Slide the stiffening into the fabric tube, ensuring it is tight. Move the seam to the centre and press open.

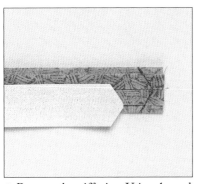

3. Remove the stiffening. Using the end of the stiffening as a template, mark the point on the fabric 6mm (¹/₄") back from one end. Stitch the point securely.

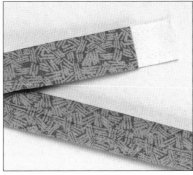

4. Clip the point and turn the fabric tube to the right side. Slide the stiffening back into the tube until the pointed end is snug. Smooth out the fabric and press.

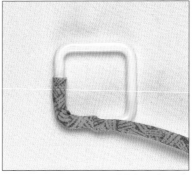

5. Self-covered buckle. Make a length of bias cut rouleau long enough to cover the buckle, adding extra to neaten the ends. Twisting the slot aside, slide the rouleau onto the buckle.

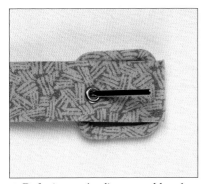

6. Referring to the diagram, add eyelets to the belt following the steps on page 79. Place the prong of the buckle from the wrong side through the eyelet at the raw end of the belt.

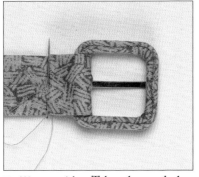

7. Wrong side. Take the underlap through the buckle, wrapping it around the bar. Fold under the raw end. Secure with handstitching on the back or machine stitching through all layers.

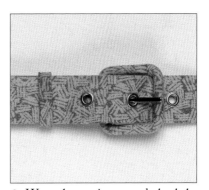

8. Wrap the carrier around the belt, allowing room for the belt to slide through. Folding one raw end under, overlap the ends and handstitch to secure.

belt keepers

To ensure belts stay at the desired position on a garment, they are usually held in place by keepers or tabs inserted into the side seams or attached to waistbands.

fabric keeper

This keeper can be set into the side seams or waistband.

Preparation. Cut lengths of fabric four times the finished width of the keeper and long enough to suit the width of the belt or waistband, adding seam allowances. It is easier to make one long strip and cut it into individual lengths.

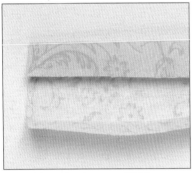

1. Making the keeper. With wrong sides together, fold the strip in half along the length and press. Unfold. Fold the raw edges to meet at the centre foldline and press.

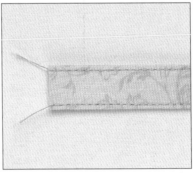

2. Refold the strip in half along the length, enclosing the raw edges. Topstitch along both sides.

3. Attaching to waistband. Prepare the waistband and facing. Matching raw edges, position the keeper on the waistband. Baste in place just inside the seam allowance.

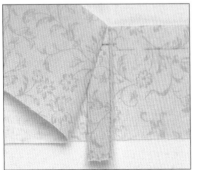

4. With right sides together and matching raw edges, pin and stitch the waistband and facing along the upper edge, sandwiching the keeper between.

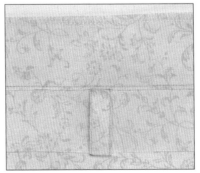

5. Trim the seam and press towards the facing. Understitch. Attach the lower edge of the waistband to the garment, sandwiching the remaining end of the keeper in the seam.

6. Alternatively, attach the waistband to the garment leaving the raw end of the keeper free. Secure the facing. Turn under the raw end of the keeper and machine stitch securely in place.

rouleau keeper

Preparation. Make a desired length of narrow rouleau following the instructions on page 119, adding seam allowances on both ends.

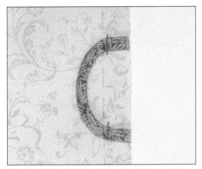

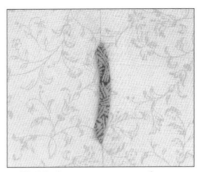

1. On the right side, pin the rouleau in position on a garment seam, spacing the ends slightly wider than the belt. Baste within the seam allowance.

2. Pin and stitch the two garment pieces together, sandwiching the keeper between.

3. Finish the seam, neaten and press.

thread keeper chain loop

Use two strands of strong thread such as topstitching or quilting thread. Cut long lengths to avoid thread joins.

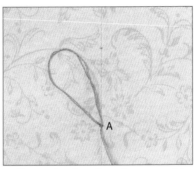

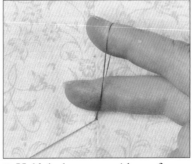

1. Secure the thread on the wrong side. Bring it to the front through the seam at A. Make a small stitch near the thread and pull through to form a loop.

2. Hold the loop open with two fingers on the right hand and the working thread with the left hand.

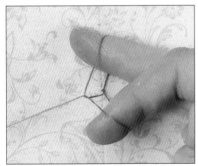

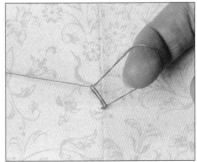

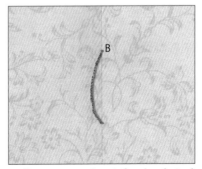

3. Holding the loop over the middle finger, hook the working thread through the loop with the index finger.

4. Release the first loop and slide it down onto the fabric.

5. Repeat steps 2 - 4 for the desired length. Take the thread through the last loop. Tighten the loop and take the thread to the back at B and secure.

belt keepers

35

detached blanket stitch loop

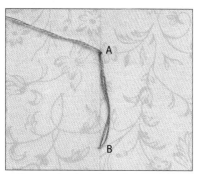

1. Secure the thread on the wrong side. Bring it to the front at A. Leaving a loose straight stitch, work several tiny back stitches at B. Return to A and secure the second long stitch as before.

2. Form a loop to the left. Slide the needle from right to left under the straight stitches and over the loop.

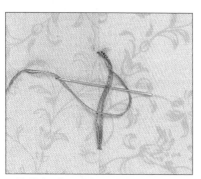

3. Pull the thread through forming a snug stitch. Form a loop to the right. Slide the needle from left to right under the stitches and over the loop.

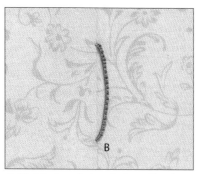

4. Finish the stitch as before. Continue alternating the blanket stitches for the length of the loop. Take the thread to the back at B and secure.

bias binding cutting strips

For the best result, cut bias binding on the true bias.

Preparation

1. The most accurate way to find the true bias is to pull a thread on both the lengthwise and crosswise grain, then fold the fabric to match the pulled thread lines. The diagonal fold created is the true bias.

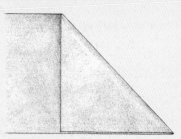

2. Press the fold and open out the fabric. Measure from the foldline and mark the width of the binding you wish to cut.

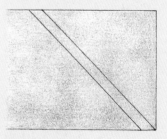

3. Leave the ends of the strips tapered or trim them at a right angle to the edge of the strip, depending on personal preference or the technique being used.

binding

Binding is used to conceal and neaten raw edges. It is a practical way to stop fraying and provides a decorative edge. Binding is folded over the edge from one side to the other and is generally the same width on the front as it is on the back. To bind a curved edge, use binding cut on the bias. This will allow it to fit the curve without twisting. Straight edges cut with the grain can be bound with tape, ribbon, braid or strips of fabric without stretch.

continuous cutting

1. Cut a large square of fabric. Fold it diagonally in half and press the fold. Unfold and cut the fabric along the foldline.

2. With right sides together, place the two triangles so the edges meet along one short side of each triangle and the long sides are at right angles. Pin.

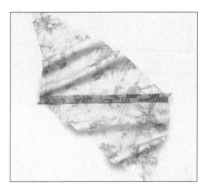

3. Stitch using a 6mm (1/4") seam allowance. Press the seam open.

4. Decide on the width of bias strip you require. Rule lines across the fabric parallel to the bias edge, keeping them evenly spaced at the required measurement.

5. With rights sides together, fold the fabric so the diagonal ends meet. Off-set the ends so the first line on one edge is aligned with the edge of the fabric.

6. Pin the ends, ensuring the lines match at the stitchline.

7. Stitch using a 6mm (1/4") seam allowance. Press the seam open.

8. Turn to the right side. Beginning at one off-set end, cut along the marked line through one layer only.

bias binding joining ends

When joining lengths of bias binding, the seam should cross the binding diagonally or it will not stretch at this point. A diagonal seam is less visible than a straight one.

Joining straight ends

1. Matching raw edges, place the ends of the bias strips right sides together and pin. Rule a line between the upper right and lower left corners. Pin, then stitch along the marked line.

2. Trim the seam and press open.

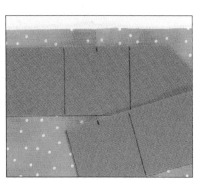

2. Measure half the width of the binding on either side of the centre marks. Rule lines at right angles to the edge across the binding to form squares. Trim excess binding.

Joining diagonal ends

1. On the wrong side, mark a 6mm (1/4") seam allowance across the ends of both strips. Place the ends right sides together, aligning the marked lines. Stitch across the end.

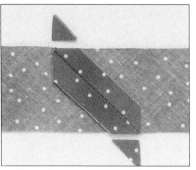

2. Press the seam open and trim the points.

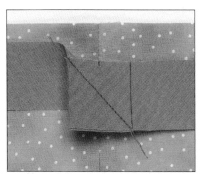

3. Rule a line between the upper left and lower right corners on the right hand end. Place the ends of the binding right sides together and pin. Stitch along the marked line.

Joining ends to form a continuous binding

This method is used when a continuous binding is required, such as a bound armhole or the outer edge of a cushion or quilt. For bias binding, the join should follow the grain of the fabric across the diagonal to give a fine finish and ensure strength and flexibility. Binding cut on the straight grain can be joined with a straight seam.

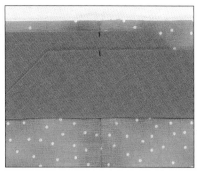

1. Leaving excess binding on both ends, pin the binding around the shape. Mark the upper edge of both ends at the centre point for the join.

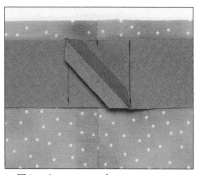

4. Trim the seam and press open.

bound edge

If your pattern has a seam allowance on the edge to be bound, trim this away before attaching the binding. The following examples can be stitched using binding cut on the bias or straight grain.

single binding

Method one is the most commonly used, but method two is most appropriate for transparent fabrics.

Preparation. To determine the width of the binding strip, decide on the finished width and multiply this by four. The width of the seam allowance is the same as the width of the binding.

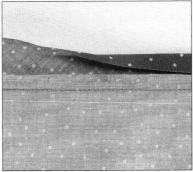

1. Press under the seam allowance along one long raw edge of the binding. With right sides together and matching raw edges, pin and stitch the unfolded edge of the binding.

2. Wrong side. Press the binding and seam away from the garment.

3. Turn the folded edge of the binding to the wrong side, enclosing the seam. Pin and handstitch the fold to the previous stitchline.

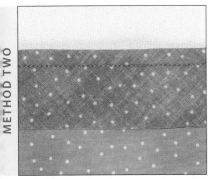

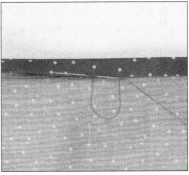

1. With right sides together and matching raw edges, pin and stitch the binding in place.

2. Wrong side. Press the binding away from the garment edge and the seam towards the garment. Fold the remaining raw edge of the binding to meet the stitchline and press the fold.

3. Fold and press the seam allowance over the raw edge of the binding. Fold the pressed binding to the wrong side enclosing the seam. Handstitch along the previous stitchline.

bound edge

double binding *also known as French binding*

Preparation. To determine the width of the binding strip for this method, decide on the finished width and multiply this by six. The width of the seam allowance is the same as the width of the binding.

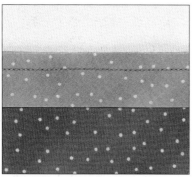

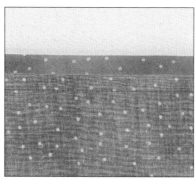

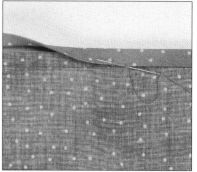

1. Fold the binding strip in half along the length and press. With right sides together and matching raw edges, pin and stitch.

2. **Wrong side.** Press the binding and seam away from the garment.

3. Fold the pressed edge to the wrong side, enclosing the seam. Pin and hand-stitch the fold to the previous stitchline.

quick binding

This method is essentially the same as the previous methods except that the binding is secured by machine stitching. Any binding can be secured by machine, either with topstitching or the method known as 'stitch in the ditch', as long as the binding has been wrapped over the seam, with the fold covering the previous stitchline. The example on page 99 shows a bound neckline using purchased bias binding.

hints **binding**

A rotary cutter is particularly useful for cutting bias binding.

Stretch bias binding very slightly as you pin it in place along concave curves, such as armholes and necklines. This will give a smoother result.

After stitching binding in place, take care not to trim away too much of the seam allowance. Enough should remain to fill the width of the binding, making it firm, smooth and less likely to buckle on the outer edge.

bound edge

40

buttonbands

Buttonbands create a tailored finish to the front opening edges of a shirt, jacket or skirt. The centre front of the garment runs down the middle of the band. Depending on the weight of the fabric, lightweight interfacing should be applied to one or both layers of the band to provide stability for the buttons and buttonholes. The two piece method provides more strength to the outer edge.

one piece method

Preparation.

Before attaching the band, stitch the hem on the lower edge of the garment. Apply interfacing to the wrong side of the buttonbands as required. Ensure you have a left and right hand band.

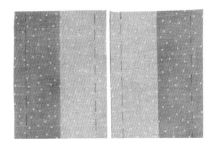

Press under the seam allowance on the long raw edge of the uninterfaced half and trim to 6mm (¼").

1. With right sides together and matching raw edges, pin and stitch the long raw edge of the band to the edge of the garment. Align the upper end with the neckline raw edge.

2. The lower end should extend past the garment hem by the width of the seam allowance.

3. Trim to the seam to 6mm (¼"). Press the band away from the garment. At the lower end, fold the band right sides together, aligning the folded edge with the seam. Stitch across the end.

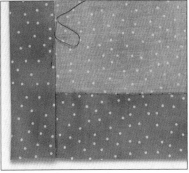

4. Trim the seam. Turn the band to the right side at the lower end and carefully push out the corner. On the wrong side, align the folded edge with the stitch-line. Pin and handstitch in place.

two piece method

Preparation. Stitch the hem on the lower edge of the garment. Apply interfacing to the wrong side of two band pieces. Press under the seam allowance on one long raw edge on the remaining two pieces.

1. With right sides together, pin and stitch a facing to a band along one long raw edge. Trim the seam and press towards the facing. Repeat for the remaining pieces. Ensure you have a left and right hand band.

2. With right sides together and matching raw edges, pin and stitch the remaining long raw edge of the band to the edge of the garment. The lower end should extend past the garment hem by the width of the seam allowance.

3. Trim the seam to 6mm (¼"). Press the band away from the garment. At the lower end, fold the band and facing right sides together, aligning the folded edge with the seam. Stitch across the lower end.

4. Trim the seam and clip the corner. Turn to the right side and finish the band following step 4 for the previous method. Topstitch on the right side, if desired.

hint horizontal or vertical buttonholes

Generally, a buttonhole is placed at right angles to the edge of the opening. Buttonbands are an exception. They should always contain vertical buttonholes parallel to the edge.

buttonholes

Standard buttonholes, horizontal or vertical, consist of two parallel rows of close machine zigzag stitch, with a bartack at each end. Some may have a rounded or keyhole end where the button sits.

Buttonholes have to withstand a lot of strain when a garment is worn, so aim to provide strength at every step. Adding interfacing behind the buttonholes will help to stabilise and strengthen the fabric.

Placement

Horizontal buttonholes are stitched at a right angle to the centre front or back line, with the first bartack just past the centre.

Vertical buttonholes follow the centre line, centred over the button position.

To ensure that an opening on a garment closes accurately, the buttonholes and the corresponding buttons must align correctly.

Pattern pieces will indicate the placement of any buttonholes required and these should be transferred to the fabric piece as part of the pattern markings.

Buttonholes are usually marked as a line with a small bar at one or both ends. The line indicates the length of the buttonhole after it is cut. The bartacks at the ends should begin at the bars, not cover them.

The length of a buttonhole should equal the diameter plus the thickness of the button being used. If you have decided on a button wider or narrower than those specified in the pattern, alter the position of the bar tack on the far end of the buttonhole, rather than the front end on horizontal buttonholes.

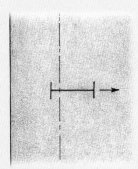

The front end is where the button sits and is positioned to close the opening with the correct overlap. For vertical buttonholes, the length should be altered evenly at both ends.

machine stitched buttonholes
automatic

This type of buttonhole is stitched using a fully automatic buttonhole presser foot. A button is placed in

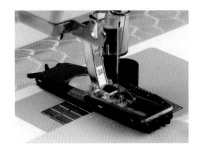

the back of the foot and the machine gauges the correct buttonhole length to fit. If the button is particularly thick, add extra length to allow for the thickness, following the instructions in your machine manual.

semi-automatic
Using the buttonhole foot and the pre-set buttonhole settings on your machine, work a buttonhole at the marked position, following the instructions in your manual. The following instructions will allow you to position buttonholes on unmarked openings, or if you have altered the spacing or placement away from the buttonhole template provided in a pattern.

HORIZONTAL BUTTONHOLE

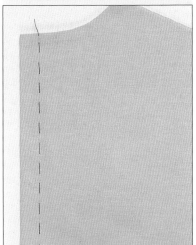

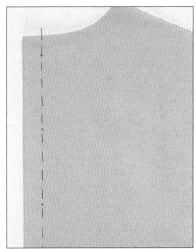

1. Determine the centre front or back position from the pattern piece. Tack a line between the upper and lower centre points. Alternatively, rule a line using a suitable fabric marker.

2. Measure from the upper edge half the button width plus 4 - 6mm ($^3/_{16}$" - $^1/_4$") and mark on the tacked line. Repeat at the lower end. Divide the distance between the marks by the number of buttons less one. Mark each point.

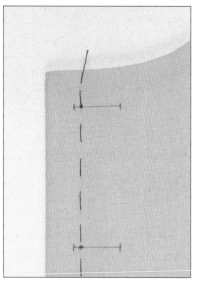

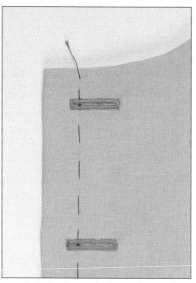

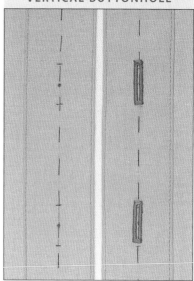

3. Beginning 3mm (¹/₈") away from the dot towards the opening edge, mark the length of a horizontal buttonhole. Move the starting point slightly forward if the button has a thick shank.

4. Stitch the buttonholes at the marked positions using the machine settings.

1. Mark the button positions following steps 1 and 2 for horizontal buttonholes, placing the upper and lower dots half the button width plus 12 - 15mm (¹/₂" - ⁵/₈") from the edge.

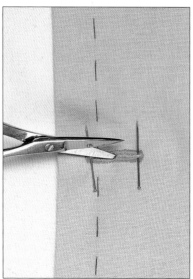

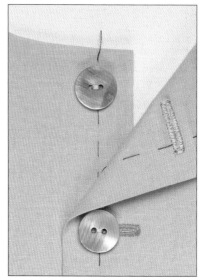

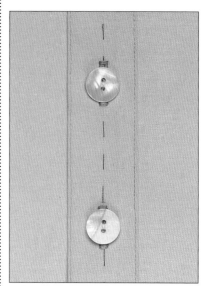

5. Push the blade of a pair of sharp pointed scissors into the centre and snip towards the ends. To prevent the bartacks being cut, place pins through the ends of the buttonhole.

6. Centring each button on a marked dot, attach the buttons following the instructions on pages 51 - 55.

2. Stitch the buttonholes using the preferred method and attach the buttons at the marked positions following the instructions on pages 51 - 55.

bound buttonhole

This style of buttonhole makes a neat, tailored alternative to the traditional stitched opening. To ensure uniformity, complete the same step on all the buttonholes before moving to the next step.

Preparation. Mark the position for the buttonhole on the right side of the fabric. Rule a line 3mm (1/8") on either side of the marked line (increase to 5mm (1/4") for thick fabrics). Extend the centre line and end bars. Cut a patch of fabric 6cm (2 3/8") wide and 2.5cm (1") longer than the finished opening. Apply interfacing and repeat the markings on the wrong side of the patch. With right sides together and matching lines, centre the patch over the marked buttonhole and pin.

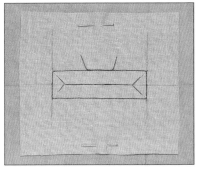

1. Using a small stitch length, stitch around the marked rectangle. Pivot at the corners and overlap the beginning. Snip along the centre and clip diagonally into each corner.

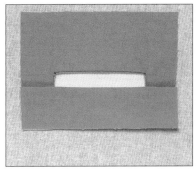

2. Wrong side. Pull the patch through to the wrong side and adjust the opening to form a rectangle. Press. Fold a pleat in the patch, aligning the fold with the centre of the opening.

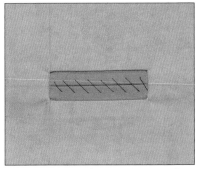

3. Repeat on the remaining edge. Adjust the pleats to ensure the binding is even on both edges. Hold the edges together with tacking. Pin the pleats together on the wrong side.

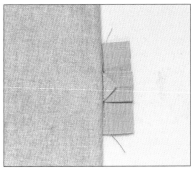

4. With the right side facing up, turn the garment edge to expose one end of the patch. Stitch across the end. Repeat at the remaining end.

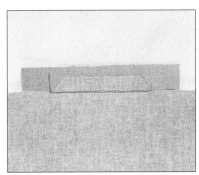

5. Repeat on the upper and lower edges, stitching just inside the original stitchline. Trim the excess fabric around the outer edge of the patch and press.

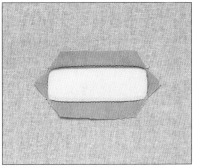

6. Facing. Mark the buttonhole on the facing. Staystitch around the opening. Clip along the centre and ends as before. Press the seam allowances to the wrong side.

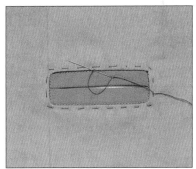

7. With wrong sides together, position the prepared facing over the back of the buttonhole and handstitch to secure.

handstitched buttonholes

Working buttonholes by hand can add a special touch to a garment. They are particularly suited to delicate fabrics but can be worked on most garments. Mark the buttonhole on the fabric, adding extra lines to mark the width. Cut the opening.

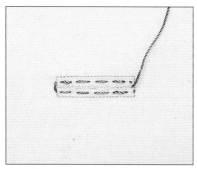

1. Work running stitch around the buttonhole finishing at the right hand end. Bring the thread to the front through the opening.

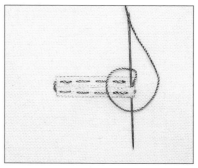

2. Take the needle through the opening and emerge on the lower line. Wrap the thread counter-clockwise behind the eye end and then the tip of the needle.

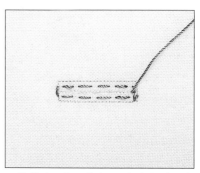

3. Pull the thread through, bringing it towards you and then up towards the opening, until the knot settles on the cut edge.

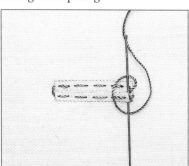

4. Take the needle through the opening again and emerge next to the previous stitch. Wrap the thread around the needle as before.

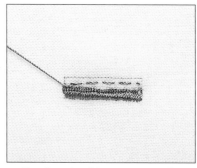

5. Continue in this manner until you reach the end of the opening. Keep the stitches as close as possible.

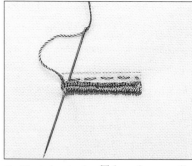

6. First bartack. Take the needle through the opening and emerge close to the previous stitch on the lower line.

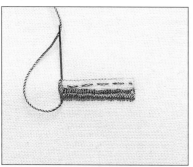

7. Work several stitches across the end. Take the needle to the back at the upper edge.

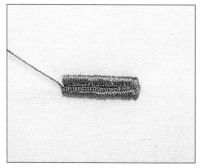

8. Turn the fabric upside down. Work buttonhole stitch as before, across the remaining long side.

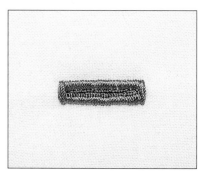

9. Make a bartack as in step 7. Take the thread through to the back, weave through the stitching and trim.

button loops

Button loops provide a decorative closure, often used for the opening of wedding gowns where the finished edge of the opening is on the centre back. Shank or ball buttons are particularly suited for this type of closure. Button loops are also a decorative way to hold the buttons on a sleeve cuff or pocket tab instead of a plain stitched buttonhole.

For a rouleau, make a test length to see if the fabric is suitable. Alternatively, use a length of narrow cord or Russia braid for the loops. Attach a button onto a scrap piece of fabric to determine the size of loop needed to slip snugly over the button. This will ensure that it holds the fabric edges together securely in the correct position.

single button loop

The instructions shown are for attaching a button loop at the top of a back opening closure, but could be adapted to any single loop wherever the application. It is often easier to attach the lining or facing to the neckline before continuing on to the back opening.

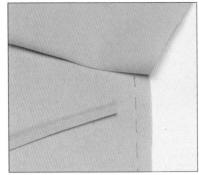

1. Mark the back opening stitchline. Make a length of rouleau following the instructions on page 119.

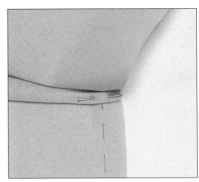

2. Matching raw edges and with the rouleau seam at the lower edge, pin one end of the rouleau just below the neck opening stitchline.

hints
single button loop

There are many other uses for fabric loops such as;

- securing the opening of a pocket or bag
- a hanging loop for an oven mitt or pot holder
- a decorative alternative to a buttonhole on a narrow sleeveband.

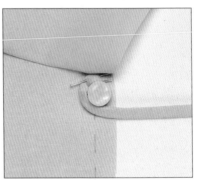

3. Centre the button on the stitchline just below the rouleau. Wrap the rouleau around the button, positioning the edge just under the button.

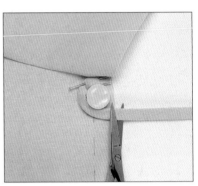

4. Trim the remaining end level with the raw edge.

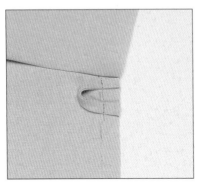

5. Pin the lower end of the rouleau in place. Remove the button and baste just inside the seam allowance.

6. Pin and stitch the facing over the garment piece, sandwiching the loop between.

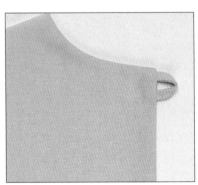

7. Trim the seam and clip the corner. Turn through to the right side and press, avoiding the loop.

continuous loops

Multiple loops can be formed directly onto the garment as described for a single loop. Depending on the size of the buttons, the loops can be placed side-by-side or spaced further apart. The smaller the buttons closer together they should be to close the garment effectively.

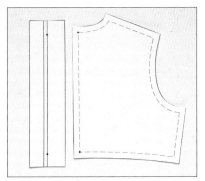

1. Cut a piece of tear-away longer than the back opening and 6cm (2 3/8") wide. Mark the centre back dots. Rule a second line 6mm (1/4") to the left of the first.

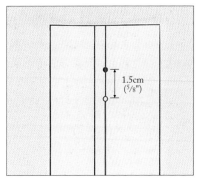

2. Mark the position for the top button on the first line, 1.5cm (5/8") from the top. Repeat at the lower end.

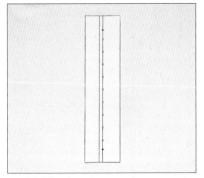

3. Divide the distance between the marks by the number of buttons minus one and mark these positions.

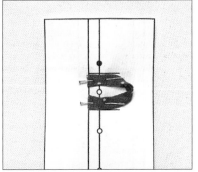

4. Aligning the raw ends with the second line, pin a length of rouleau at the top button position following step 3 of the single loop. Mark the edge above and below and remove the rouleau.

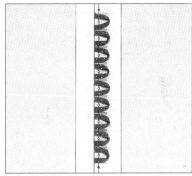

5. Mark the same distances at each button position. Cut strips of rouleau for each button. Pin a length at each position, aligning the marks. Baste to the tear-away template.

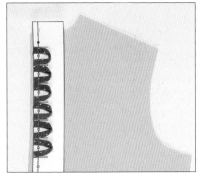

6. Matching centre lines, place the template on the right side of the back opening with the loops facing into the garment. Baste the loops in place and then tear away the template.

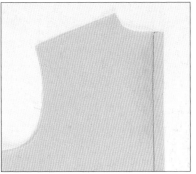

7. With right sides together, place the facing or lining, over the loops. Pin together horizontally and stitch just inside the basting.

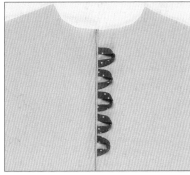

8. Trim the seam and press the facing and seam away from the garment. Understitch along the facing. Press the facing to the wrong side, taking care to avoid the loops.

button loops

49

purchased loop tape

Cut a length of the tape to fit the opening, plus two extra loops. Pull out one loop at each end, leaving the tails of the elastic cord.

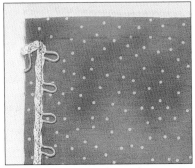

1. With the loops facing inwards, position the edge of the tape just inside the stitchline. Fold excess tape at the ends into the seam allowance. Baste along the edge of the tape, securing the tails.

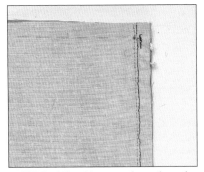

2. With right sides together, place the facing or lining over the loops. Pin and stitch just inside the basting.

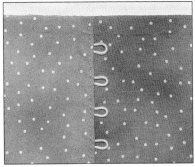

3. Press the facing and seam away from the garment. Understitch along the facing.

4. Press the facing to the wrong side, taking care to avoid the loops.

thread loop

When a front or back button closure is fastened correctly, a small flap of the bodice will extend beyond the first button. Attaching a tiny button and thread loop adds the perfect finishing touch. Use doubled thread in a colour to match the fabric. The distance between A and B is slightly less than the width of the button. Alternating the direction of the blanket stitches, will prevent the loop from twisting.

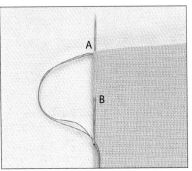

1. Bring the thread to the front through the top seam at A. Make a few tiny stitches to secure the thread. Slide the needle between the layers from B to A.

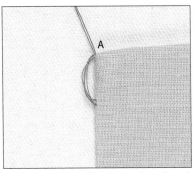

2. Repeat step 1, forming a four thread loop. Test the loop with the button and adjust if necessary. Secure the thread at A with a few tiny stitches.

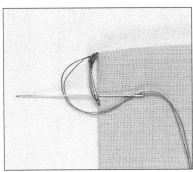

3. Begin to work detached blanket stitches around the thread loop.

button loops

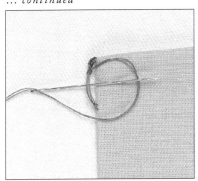

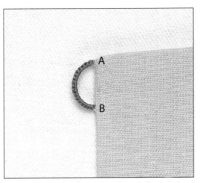

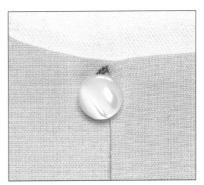

4. On each alternate stitch, work the blanket stitch in the opposite direction.

5. Work blanket stitches alternating from side to side, pulling firmly towards A. When the loop is covered, secure the thread at B.

6. Attach the button to correspond with the loop.

buttons

The method of attaching a button depends on the style of the button.

Preparation

Mark the positions for the buttons after the buttonholes have been stitched and cut open.

1. Overlap the two sections of the garment, aligning the centre lines. Place a pin through the buttonhole and into the underlap.

2. Ease the pin through the buttonhole without removing it from the fabric. Mark the button position on the centre line level with the pin.

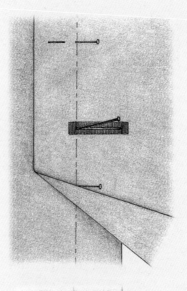

attaching buttons by machine

Machine stitching is a quick way to attach buttons, especially if there are a great number. Because the stitching can be easily unravelled, the thread ends should be finished by hand. Mark the centre line and the position of the buttons with tacking at right angles to each other. Stitch the buttons in place following the instructions in your manual.

buttons

51

handstitching
flat buttons

When the button is attached, it is advisable to create a thread shank behind the button, especially on thicker fabrics. This allows the overlapping fabric to fit under the button without puckering.

The thicker the fabric, the longer the shank needs to be.

A matchstick or toothpick can be used as a spacer when creating the shank. Alternatively keep the stitches loose but even.

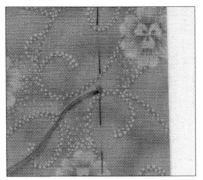

1. Two hole. Mark the position for the button on the fabric. Secure a double sewing thread at the marked position.

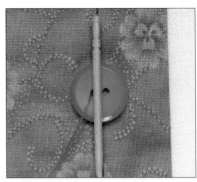

2. Take the thread through the left hand hole in the button and centre it over the marked point. Place a spacer, over the button between the holes.

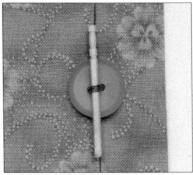

3. Stitch the button in place with several stitches over the spacer, working through the same holes in the fabric. Finish with the thread on the back.

4. Bring the thread to the front between the fabric and the button. Remove the spacer.

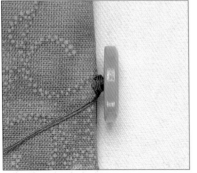

5. Wrap the thread around the stitching five or six times to create the shank.

6. Take the thread to the back and secure.

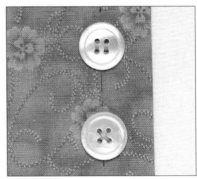

7. Four hole. Stitch through the holes in the same manner, working in straight pairs or in the form of a cross.

handstitching reinforced button

Stitching a small reinforcing button on the wrong side behind the main button provides strength at points of great strain. They take the stress that would otherwise be on the fabric. Both buttons must have the same number of holes. If the fabric is delicate, or in an area that can't be interfaced, substitute the button for a doubled square of fabric or reinforcing tape.

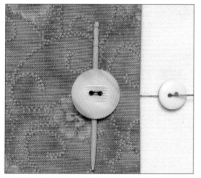

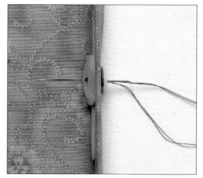

1. Begin to attach the main button, using a spacer. Place a small button on the wrong side directly behind the main button.

2. Continue to attach the buttons, taking the needle through the holes in both buttons. Finish by taking the thread to the front and complete the shank. End off the thread by taking it through the shank several times.

handstitching shank buttons

Mark the position for the button on the fabric and secure the doubled thread at this point. Place the button over the marked point with the shank parallel to the buttonhole position.
Stitch the button in place, taking the needle through the fabric close to the base of the shank.

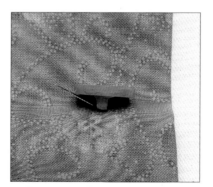

hints shank buttons

If the shank on the chosen button isn't high enough for the fabric thickness, add a little height by working a thread shank when attaching it.

Avoid using buttons with a high shank on the back of garments intended for babies or toddlers, as the shank will press into the child's back when laying down.

buttons

attaching buttons with embroidery

Bullion buds are a decorative way of attaching a four hole button. Using your chosen embroidery thread, secure the thread on the back and position the button so that the holes form a diamond.

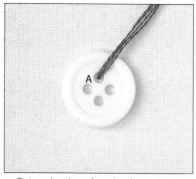

1. Bring the thread to the front through the upper hole (A).

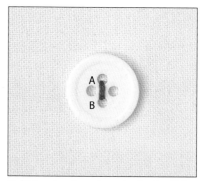

2. Take the thread to the back of the fabric through the lower hole (B). Pull the thread firmly to anchor the button.

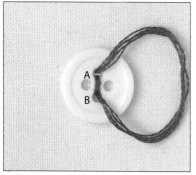

3. Emerge at A. Take the needle to the back at B. Pull the thread through, leaving a large loop on the front.

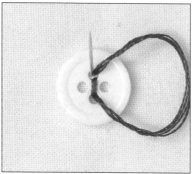

4. Re-emerge at A and leave the needle in the button. Hold the needle firmly on the back of the fabric.

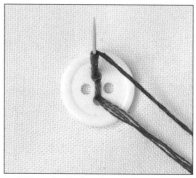

5. Wrap the loop of thread around the needle in a clockwise direction for the required number of wraps. Ensure they are evenly packed together.

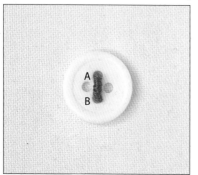

6. Holding the wraps securely, carefully pull the thread through. Pull the thread towards you until the wraps are even and lie firmly against the button. Take the thread to the back at B and secure.

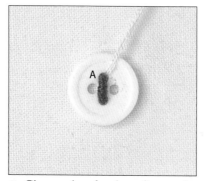

7. Change thread colour. Secure the thread on the back and emerge at A, just to the right of the inner petal.

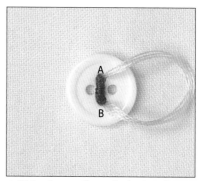

8. Take the needle to the back at B, just to the right of the inner petal. Pull the thread through leaving a large loop on the front as before.

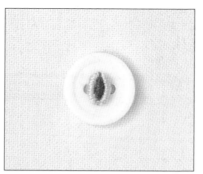

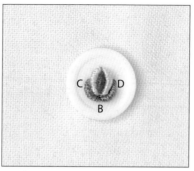

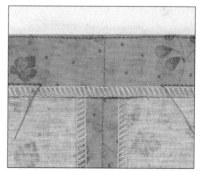

9. Work the bullion knot in the same manner as before. Ensure it lies to the right of the inner petal.

10. Stitch a bullion knot on the left of the inner petal in the same manner to complete the bud.

11. Change thread colour. Work bullion knots from C to B and from D to B for leaves. Secure the thread.

casings

A casing is a tunnel formed on a garment to enclose elastic or a drawstring. All casings should be slightly wider than the elastic or the drawstring, to allow for free movement. Casings can be either folded or applied. Folded casings are made using an allowance given on the pattern and applied casings are formed using a separate piece of fabric. A folded casing is usually restricted to straight edges, but can cope with a gentle curve if they are not too wide.

A facing can also be attached to make an applied casing. This method is best suited to casings required on curves, as the facing can be a piece of fabric cut on the bias or purchased bias binding. Elastic should be a firm, corded type in a width to suit the casing. Non-roll elastic is used for waistbands to ensure the casing stays flat.

Cut a length of elastic slightly less than the circumference of the body where the casing sits, such as the waist or wrist, plus 2cm (³⁄₄") for an overlap to join the ends.

folded casing with elastic

1. Neaten the raw edge with a zigzag or overlock stitch, or press under 6mm (1/4"). Fold the casing to the wrong side for the required depth and pin.

2. Leaving an opening at a seam, stitch along the neatened edge to secure the casing. The folded edge may also be topstitched to hold the elastic firmly in the casing.

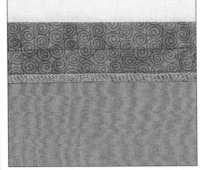

folded casing with frill

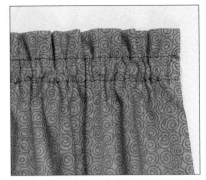

3. Attach a safety pin to one end of the elastic. Secure the other end to the fabric near the opening to stop it slipping into the casing. Work the elastic through the casing using the safety pin.

1. Leaving the ends open or an opening at a seam, fold and stitch the lower edge of the casing as before. Work another line of stitching above the first to create the casing.

2. Thread elastic through the casing and finish as required. The upper section of the casing forms the frill.

drawstring casing

Stitch buttonholes in the centre of the casing, before it is folded and stitched. Make the casing and insert the drawstring through the buttonholes.

4. Ensuring the elastic isn't twisted within the casing, overlap the ends and pin. Stitch a square with a cross in the middle on the overlap, or work zigzag stitching to secure the ends.

partial casing

Partial casings can be used at the back or sides of garments. Fold and stitch the casing following the instructions for folded casing, leaving the ends open. Take the elastic through the casing, securing the ends with stitching just inside the seam allowance.

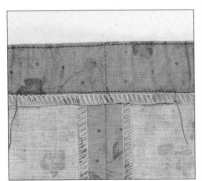

5. Pull the ends back into the casing. Reposition the edges of the opening and stitch closed.

applied casings

An applied casing is a strip of fabric attached to a flat area where there is no seam to form a casing. It may be stitched onto the right or wrong side. A separate piece of fabric can also be applied on the upper edge of pants and skirts, or the lower edge of a sleeve as shown on page 135. This is called a faced casing and is useful to reduce bulk when the garment is made from a heavyweight fabric.

Preparation

Cut a piece of fabric the same width as the elastic or band, adding 6mm (¼") to allow for ease through the casing and seam allowance on both sides. The length of the fabric strip is determined by the length at the point where the casing is applied, plus seam allowance at each end.

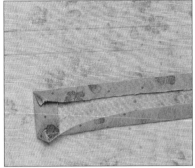

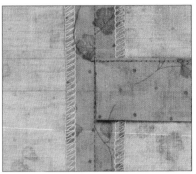

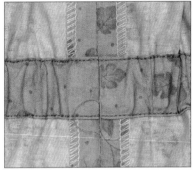

1. Continuous casing. Press under the seam allowance at each end of the strip and then the upper and lower edges. Mark the casing centre line on the garment. Mark a second line half the width of the finished casing, above the first.

2. Pin and stitch the casing strip to the garment, aligning the upper edge with the second line.

3. When you return to the starting point, butt the two ends together. Follow steps 3 - 5 on page 56 to insert the elastic. Handstitch the opening closed.

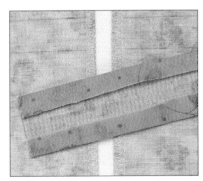

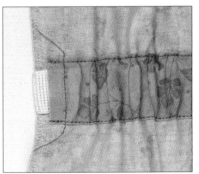

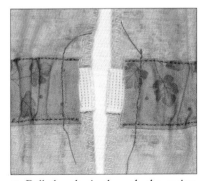

4. Open casing. Press under the seam allowance of the fabric strip on the upper and lower edges only. Mark the centre and upper placement line of the casing as before.

5. Pin and stitch the casing in place. Pin one end of the elastic near one end of the casing. Take the elastic through the casing and baste the end just inside the seam allowance to secure.

6. Pull the elastic through the casing and secure the remaining end as before.

casings

clipping and notching

After stitching a seam on a curved edge, the seam allowance must be clipped to allow it to lie flat behind the seam when turned to the right side. Use small sharp pointed scissors and take care to finish the cut within a few fabric threads of the stitching. If the clip is too close, the seam may fray at this point.

See also; Clipping concave and convex curves when one is stitched to the other on page 72; Clipping corners on page 127.

concave curves clipping

Concave or inward facing curves such as necklines or faced armholes, spread open when turned to lie in the opposite direction.

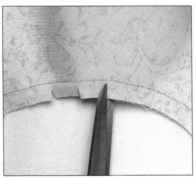

1. Clipping requires a straight cut into the seam allowance at a right angle to the stitching.

2. When the seam is turned to the right side, the seam allowance spreads at the cut to lie flat.

convex curves notching

Convex or outward facing curves such as the outer edge of a round collar, will compress when turned to the inside.

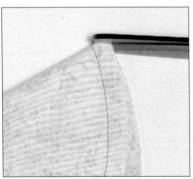

1. Fold the seam allowance at a right angle to the stitching and cut diagonally towards the stitching.

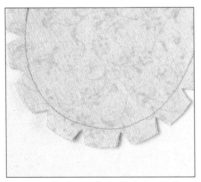

2. A small triangular notch is cut into the seam. The tighter the curve, the wider and closer the notches.

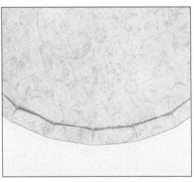

3. Wrong side. When the seam is turned to the right side, the notch closes up, allowing the seam allowance to lie flat.

scallops

1. At the peak of a scallop, clip toward the peak, ending close to the stitching.

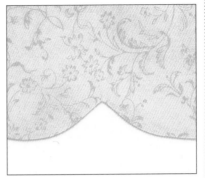

2. When turned to the right side, the clip opens out allowing the seam to sit flat on the inside.

partial seams

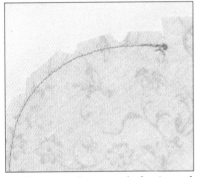

1. If a seam ends at a marked point and the remainder of the seam allowance is required for a further step, clip to the marked point close to the stitching.

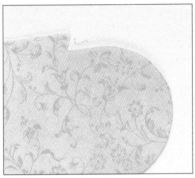

2. When turned to the right side, the seam allowance remains intact, extending beyond the finished edge.

hems

1. To reduce bulk in a hem or facing, clip the seam at the fold. Press the seam within the hem in the opposite direction to the main seam.

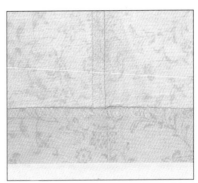

2. Fold the hem on the foldline. The seam lies flat inside the hem. This method is not recommended for sheer fabrics.

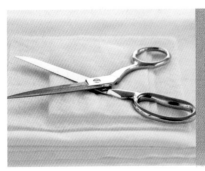

hints clipping

Clip or notch a seam before trimming any excess, except when the seam requires grading. In that instance, grade first, then clip or notch.

When clipping any curve, the distance between the clips will depend on the tightness of the curve. The tighter the curve, the closer the clips or notches should be.

collars

Collars are often the most noticeable style element on a garment and are designed in many forms. They fall into three main groups; stand, flat and rolled. The main factor in determining which group a collar falls into is the relationship between the neckline curve on the garment to that on the collar.

The styling of collars doesn't affect its basic construction because they commonly consist of two parts, the upper and under collar, or the collar and collar facing.

An important element to any collar is the interfacing used to define and support the shape. It is vital that the weight of the interfacing should balance the weight of the fabric being used. Interfacing is generally applied to the wrong side of the under collar, but as with any rule, there can be exceptions. Interfacing the upper collar can also provide stability for embroidery or other forms of embellishment. If constructing a collar from a very lightweight or pale fabric, apply interfacing to the wrong side of the upper collar. This prevents the seams from showing through on the right side.

hint corners

To define a corner, take a knotted thread through the collar and out at the corner. Pull on the thread to ease the corner out.

flat collar

The neckline curve of a flat collar is very similar to the neckline edge of the garment, causing the collar to roll slightly and fall flat across the shoulder. The two collar pieces should be an exact mirror image of each other to achieve a balanced result. If the garment has a front opening, a flat collar is usually constructed in one piece that meets at the centre front.

For a back opening garment, the collar may have two pieces, with the ends meeting at the centre front and back.

hint collars

To make the collar seams roll to the back, trim 2mm (¹⁄₁₆") from the neckline seam of the under collar. Match raw edges when tacking along the neckline.

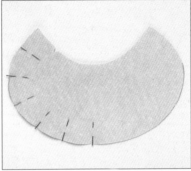

1. Apply interfacing to the wrong side of the under collar. Matching raw edges, pin the upper and under collar pieces right sides together, leaving the neck edge open.

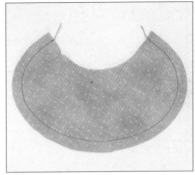

2. Stitch the collar seam.

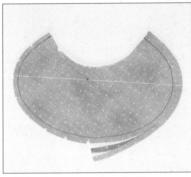

3. Trim the seam and grade if necessary. Notch the curves.

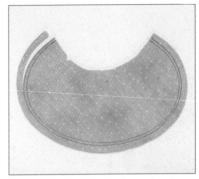

3a. Alternatively stitch again 3mm (¹⁄₈") away from the first stitchline, within the seam allowance. Trim close to the second line of stitching.

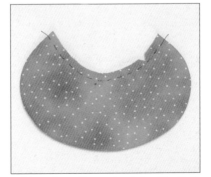

4. Turn the collar to the right side. Roll the seam slightly towards the under collar and press lightly. Tack the raw edges together at the neckline.

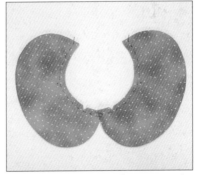

5. Two piece collar. Construct the second half of the collar in the same manner. Secure the two pieces where they meet on the neckline, basting just inside the stitchline.

collars

rolled collar

The neckline curve on the collar is often flat or slightly curved in the opposite direction to the garment. When attached, the collar stands high at the centre back (the stand) then rolls to fall towards the shoulders (the fall). The fold between the stand and the fall is the roll line.

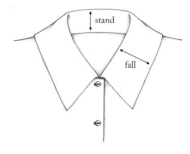

one piece rolled collar

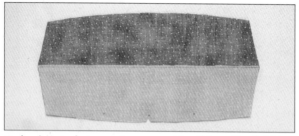

1. Apply interfacing to the wrong side of the collar finishing at, or 2mm ($^1/_8$") past, the foldline. The interfaced section will be the under collar.

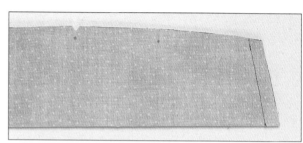

2. Fold the collar right sides together, matching raw edges. Stitch across the ends.

3. Trim the seams and clip the corners.

4. Turn to the right side. Push out the corners and roll the seams slightly towards the under collar. Matching centres, pin and tack the raw edges together at the neckline. Press lightly.

two piece rolled collar

A rolled collar with a shaped edge will need to be constructed from two separate pieces.

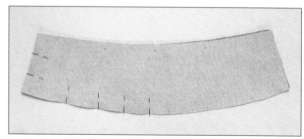

1. Apply interfacing to the wrong side of the under collar. With right sides together, pin the upper and under collar pieces, leaving the neck edges open.

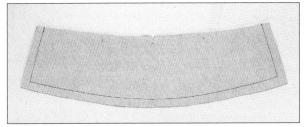

2. Stitch around the collar, pivoting at the corners.

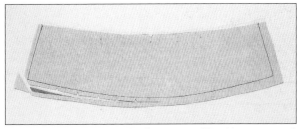

3. Trim the seam and grade if necessary. Clip the corners and notch the curve.

4. Turn the collar to the right side, rolling the seam slightly towards the underside. Push out the corners carefully. Lightly press.

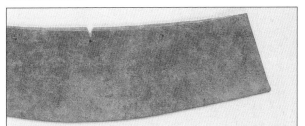

5. Tack the raw edges together at the neckline. Rolling the lower seam under may make a small difference in the position of the raw edges at the upper edge.

stand collar

Simple stand collars rise up from the neckline. Mandarin or Nehru collars are both examples of stand collars.

basic stand collar

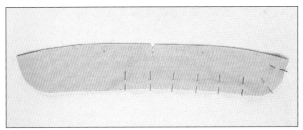

1. Apply interfacing to the wrong side of the under collar. Pin the upper and under collar pieces right sides together, leaving the neck edge open.

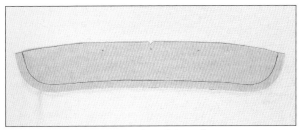

2. Stitch around the outer edge of the collar.

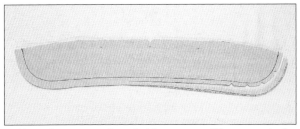

3. Trim the seam and grade if necessary. Clip or notch the curves.

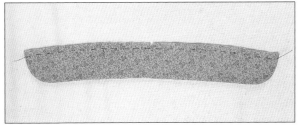

4. Turn the collar to the right side, rolling the seam to the edge. Tack the raw edges together at the neckline. Press lightly.

shirt collar

The shirt collar has
two parts, the stand
and the collar.
The two sections are usually
separate pieces but they can be
designed as one.

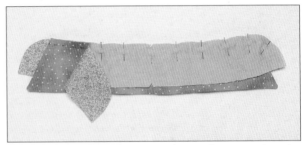

1. Construct a rolled collar following the steps on page 62. Apply interfacing to the wrong side of one stand piece.

2. Matching centres, edges and markings, pin the collar with the interfaced layer facing the uninterfaced stand piece.

3. Tack in place. Matching raw edges and centres, place the interfaced stand piece over the collar and pin.

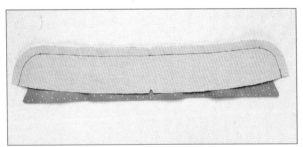

4. Stitch. Trim the seam. Clip and notch the curves of the stand.

5. Turn the collar to the right side, rolling the seam to the edge on the ends of the stand. Press the collar away from the seam. Matching centres, tack the raw edges together.

shawl collar

A shawl collar is a variation of a rolled collar. A shawl collar can be narrow or quite wide and can be used on shirts, jackets, coats and dressing gowns, giving a soft unbroken line between the collar and the lapels.

A shawl collar is often used in conjunction with a wrapped front opening, having a soft tie belt to hold the front together, rather than a traditional button closure.

Preparation. Apply interfacing to the wrong side of the complete collar and front facing piece, omitting the hem area at the lower edges. Staystitch around the corners between the collar and the shoulder seam.

Clip diagonally into the corner on both pieces.

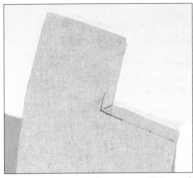

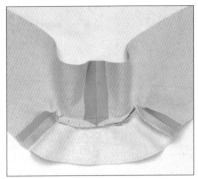

1. Garment shoulder seams. Pin and stitch the front pieces to the back, ending securely where the stitchlines meet at the neckline. Neaten both sides of the seam separately and press open.

2. Garment back neckline. Pin and stitch the centre back collar seam. Press the seam open. Matching seam with centre back, pin and stitch across the back neckline. Clip the curve.

3. Collar and back neckline facing. Stitch the shoulder seams following step 1. Complete the collar and facing following step 2. Neaten the outer edge of the facing.

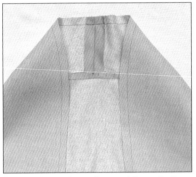

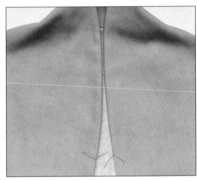

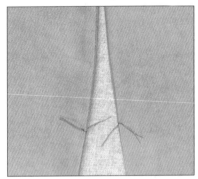

4. Attaching the collar and front facing. With right sides together, matching centres and markings, pin the collar piece to the garment. Stitch in place, stitching each side from the centre back to the hem.

5. Trim the seam and clip the curves. Turn to the right side and finger press the seam. Referring to the pattern, mark the point on both sides of the front where the collar will begin to roll.

6. Press the front opening edges lightly, rolling the collar seam towards the garment between the marks and placing it on the edge below the marks.

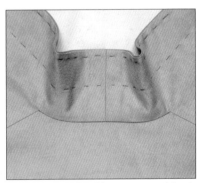

7. Tack through all layers along the roll line and close to the outer edge.

8. Matching shoulder seams and back neckline, pin the layers together. Stitch in the ditch from shoulder to shoulder across the back.

9. Handstitch the edge of the facing to the shoulder seams. Finish the lower edge of the facings following the instructions on page 93.

collars

collars – attaching

There are three main methods of attaching a collar to a neckline - using a continuous facing or lining, using a facing on both sides of the opening edge only or applying the collar directly to the neckline. The instructions show a different collar for each method, but the method isn't limited to the collar style depicted.

continuous facing or lining

Preparation. Construct your chosen collar. Staystitch the neckline on the garment pieces. Apply interfacing to the wrong side of the back and front facings. Stitch and finish the shoulder seams in the garment and the facings. Neaten the outer edge of the facing.

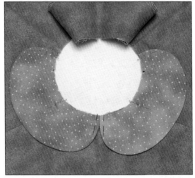

1. Matching raw edges, centres and shoulder marks, pin the collar to the neckline.

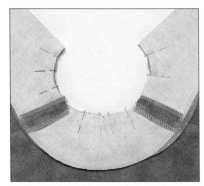

2. Baste the collar in place. Matching raw edges, centres and seams, pin the facing over the neckline, sandwiching the collar between.

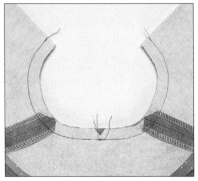

3. Beginning at the centre back, stitch the neckline seam through all layers. Return to the centre back and stitch the remainder of the seam.

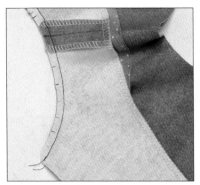

4. Trim the seam and grade if necessary. Clip the curve and the corners.

5. Press the seam towards the facing. Understitch close to the seam on the facing.

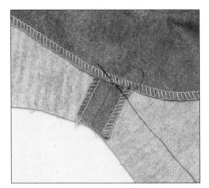

6. Turn the facing to the inside of the garment. Matching seams, handstitch in position on the shoulder seams.

front facings only

Preparation

Construct your chosen collar. Staystitch the neckline on the garment pieces. Apply interfacing to the wrong side of the front facings. Stitch and finish the shoulder seams in the garment. Neaten the outer edge of the facings. Press under the seam allowances on the shoulder edges of the facings. Cut a length of bias binding 5cm (2") wide.

The length of the binding is determined by the measurement across the back neck plus 2cm (³⁄₄") at each end. Fold the binding in half along the length and press.

METHOD ONE

1. Matching raw edges and centre front and back marks, pin and tack the collar to the neckline.

2. Matching raw edges and the folded edge on each facing to the garment shoulder seams, pin front facings to the neckline. The ends of the collar are sandwiched between. Baste the facings and collar in place.

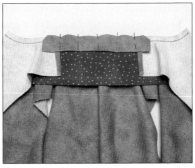

3. Matching raw edges, pin the binding across the back neck and over the ends of the facings. Stitch through all layers.

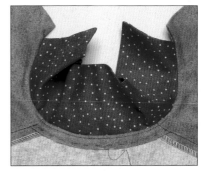

4. Trim the seam, clip the curve and the corners. Turn to the right side and understitch on the facing and binding. Handstitch the binding to the neckline and the facing to the shoulder seams.

METHOD TWO

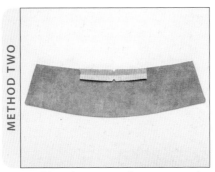

1. Clip the seam allowance to the marked shoulder points on the upper collar. Tack the raw edges together on the front sections of the collar, folding the clipped seam allowances back.

2. With right sides together, pin the undercollar in place, matching seams and marks. Tack the collar to the neckline from the ends to the clipped points. Tack the under collar only across the back neckline.

collars

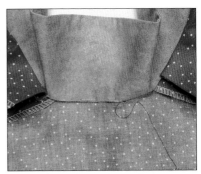

3. Pin the front facings over the neckline, sandwiching the ends of the collar. Keeping the uppercollar seam allowance folded back between the clips, stitch around the neckline.

4. Trim the seam, clip the curve and corners. Clip the seam allowance, level with the ends of the facings. Turn the facings to the right side.

5. Trim the folded seam allowance on the uppercollar. Press the back neckline seams towards the collar. Align the fold with the previous stitchline. Pin and handstitch. Secure the facings.

attaching a stand collar

Preparation. Construct your chosen collar. Leave the raw edges free at the neckline. Staystitch the neckline on the garment pieces. Stitch and finish the shoulder seams. Finish the front opening edges with facings or buttonbands.

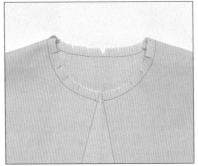

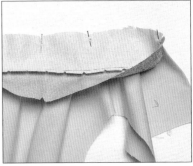

1. Clip the neckline at approximately 2cm (³/₄") intervals. This will allow the collar to fit smoothly onto the neckline.

2. With right sides together and matching raw edges and markings, pin and tack the raw edge of the interfaced stand to the neckline.

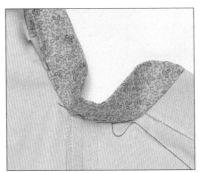

3. Stitch the seam, securing the ends. Trim and grade if necessary.

4. Press seam towards stand. Press under seam allowance on remaining raw edge and trim to 6mm (¹/₄"). Matching marks, align folded edge with the previous stitchline. Pin and handstitch.

5. Press. On the right side of the stand, topstitch close to the edge if desired.

collars

Corners

Producing a beautifully finished corner is a combination of careful stitching, clipping, turning and pressing. The method used will depend on the weight of the fabric and the angle of the corner.

On finishing edges, such as hems and bindings, the corners are best formed using mitring techniques; either folded or stitched, or a combination of both.

stitching a corner seam

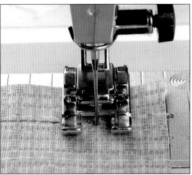

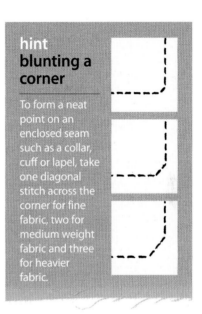

1. Stitch the seam towards the corner. Stop with the needle down at the corner point. The distance to the front edge of the fabric should equal the seam allowance.

2. With the needle in the fabric, lift the presser foot. Pivot the fabric until the adjacent raw edge is aligned with the guide. Lower the presser foot and continue.

hint
blunting a corner

To form a neat point on an enclosed seam such as a collar, cuff or lapel, take one diagonal stitch across the corner for fine fabric, two for medium weight fabric and three for heavier fabric.

attaching inner to outer corners

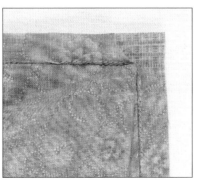

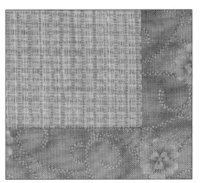

1. Staystitch the inner corner just inside the seam allowance. Clip to the point, taking care not to cut the stitching.

2. Spread the clipped section to fit the outer corner. Match raw edges and pin. With the clipped side uppermost, stitch the seam, pivoting at the corner.

3. Press the seam towards the clipped fabric.

box corner Form this corner in the same manner if there are seams on both edges.

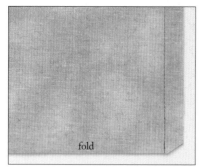

1. Fold the fabric, right sides together and stitch the side seam. Clip the corner almost to the stitching.

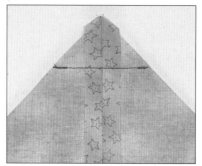

2. Press the seam open. Refold the fabric, matching the seam to the previous foldline. At the required measurement, pin and stitch at a right angle to the previous seam.

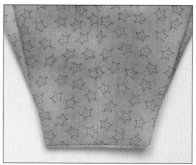

3. Trim away the point if necessary and neaten the seam. Turn to the right side.

corners – finishing mitring turned hem

This mitred corner makes a neat finish when hemming a right angled corner. The hem must be the same depth on both sides of the corner. It might be used to secure the hem and front opening of an unlined jacket, the corner of a hem or the side vent of a shirt. For quilts, blankets and placemats, this would make the perfect method to attach a lining while finishing the outer edge at the same time.

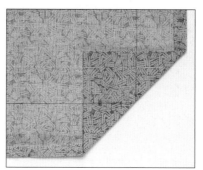

1. Neaten the raw edges using the preferred method. Press under the required hem allowance on both sides and unfold. Fold the corner diagonally, aligning the foldlines. Press.

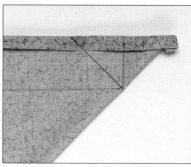

2. Unfold the corner. Fold the corner on the bias, right sides together and matching neatened edges. Stitch along the diagonal fold.

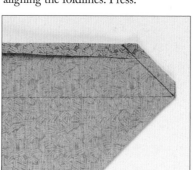

3. Trim the seam, leaving a 6mm (1/4") seam allowance. Clip the point.

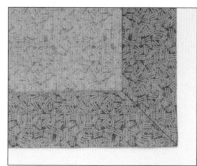

4. Press the seam open. Turn to the right side. Tack the hems in place. Handstitch to secure or topstitch on the right side, pivoting at the corner.

mitring binding

These instructions apply to both single and double binding. The following steps are worked using a double binding.

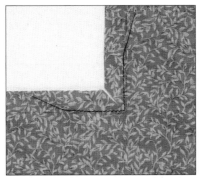

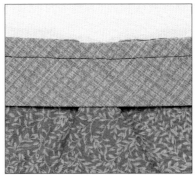

INNER CORNER. 1. Staystitch the corner just inside the seam allowance. Clip into the corner almost up to the stitching.

2. Press the binding in half along the length. Spread the cut corner. With right sides together, pin the binding to the edge. Stitch along the stitchline.

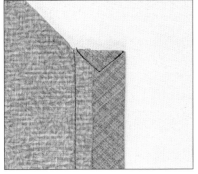

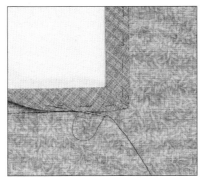

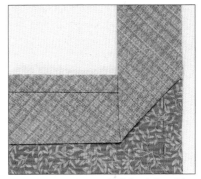

3. Fold the binding right sides together at the corner. Stitch from the seam to the outer corner in a 'V' shape, slightly more shallow than the width of the binding.

4. Trim the seam and clip into the point. Fold the binding over the seam allowance. Pin, tack and handstitch the binding in place along the previous stitchline.

OUTER CORNER. 1. With right sides together, pin and stitch the binding along the stitchline, ending securely at the seam turning point. Fold the binding diagonally from the corner, covering the previous stitching. Press the diagonal fold.

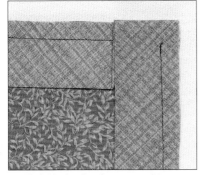

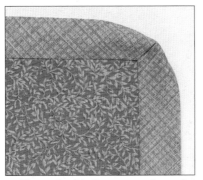

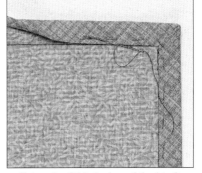

2. Refold the binding, matching raw edges on the second edge. The upper fold should be at a right angle to the point. From the corner point, pin and stitch along the second edge.

3. Press the binding away from the fabric. Fold the binding over the seam allowance to the wrong side, forming a mitre at the corner on the right side.

4. Bring the folded edge of the binding to match the previous stitchline, forming a mitre at the corner on the wrong side. Pin, tack and handstitch in place along the previous stitchline.

curves

similar curves

When joining similar curves, such as the crotch of a pair of pants, a section of the seam may be on the bias. As this may be strained during wear, stitches can break unless care is taken when stitching the seam. The longer the stitch, the more likely it is to break.

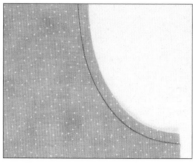

1. With right sides together, pin and stitch the two pieces with a small machine stitch. Stitch the tightest part of the curve again.

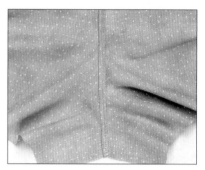

2. Trim the seam and neaten. Press the seam to one side.

convex to concave curve

Stitching two pieces together with dissimilar curves, such as a princess seam running over the bust, requires careful marking, pinning and clipping to ensure the seam follows the contours of the body. Refer to page 58 for clipping and notching.

1. Staystitch the concave curve just inside the seam allowance. Clip the tightest section.

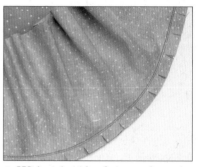

2. With right sides facing and matching markings, pin the two pieces together. Spread the clipped edge slightly to fit the curve. Tack. Stitch with the clipped side facing up.

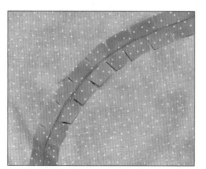

3. Trim the seam and finger press open. Notch the fullness on the convex curve, offsetting the clips and notches wherever possible.

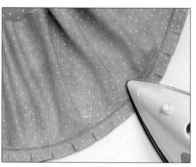

4. Press flat with the point of the iron. Take care not to press into the garment.

5. Press the seam open over a curved surface, moving the seam to keep the curves aligned.

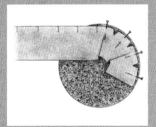

darts

Darts are used to shape flat fabric, enabling a garment to follow the curves of the body. They occur mostly on women's clothing to contour the bust, waist and hips. The pattern will indicate in which direction to press the dart. Horizontal darts are pressed downwards and vertical darts are most commonly pressed towards the centre.

basic dart

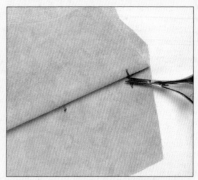

1. Mark the darts with tailor's tacks following the instructions on page 23.

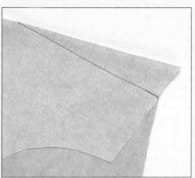

2. Matching the tacks, fold the dart and pin. Stitch the dart from the outer edge towards the point. Secure the stitching at the point by stitching backwards for approximately 1cm (3/8").

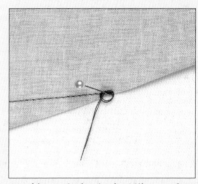

2a. Alternatively, tie the tails together. Tighten the knot, adjusting it with a pin to settle on the fabric.

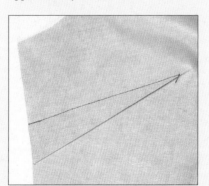

3. Press the dart flat first to set the stitching. Press the dart to one side as indicated on the pattern.

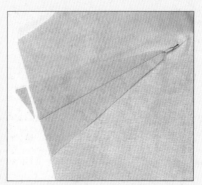

3a. Thick fabrics. Cut the dart to within 1.5cm (5/8") of the point. Trim the sides and press open.

curves | darts

contour dart

A contour dart is often long and shapes the fabric at the waist of a garment. It has a point at each end and the widest part at the centre.

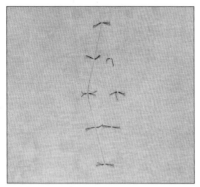

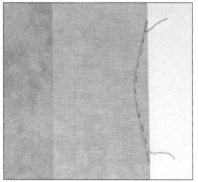

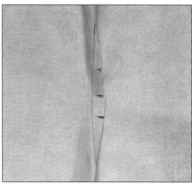

1. Transfer all the pattern markings for the dart with tailors' tacks following the instructions on page 23.

2. With right sides together and matching marks, fold the dart along the centre. Pin and tack. Stitch the dart securing as before.

3. Remove the tacking. Clip the dart to 3mm ($1/8$") from the stitching so the fold lays flat. Press the dart to one side.

french dart

A French dart appears on the front of a garment extending from the hip or waist side seam to the bust.

A French dart is wider than a basic dart and therefore must be cut to open the centre before stitching.

If curved, the upper line is shorter than the lower and the two must be eased to fit.

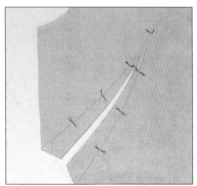

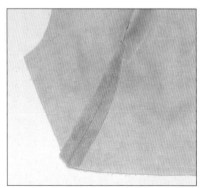

1. Transfer the pattern markings including the centre cut line. Remove the pattern and cut the dart.

2. With right sides together and matching stitchlines and marks, pin and tack. Stitch the dart starting at the outer edge, securing at the point.

3. Remove the tacking. Trim and press the dart open.

easing

Easing occurs when attaching two edges of differing lengths, such as fitting the shoulder cap of a sleeve into the armhole. The longer edge is eased to fit the shorter one. Small amounts of ease can be accommodated with careful pinning, but areas of greater ease will require a row of machine stitching just inside the seam allowance to control fullness.

Pin easing

When pinning out a small amount of ease, refer to the following steps, omitting the row of machine easing. Pin at the ends and centres first, matching edges, seams or markings. Working from the centre of each segment, pin to distribute the ease until the pins are 2cm (¾") apart. Baste close to the stitchline before stitching.

machine easing

Preparation

Stitch a row of machine easing just inside the stitchline of the longer piece. Mark the centre of the area to be eased on the edge of both fabric pieces.

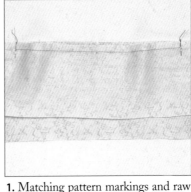

1. Matching pattern markings and raw edges, pin the fabrics together at each end of the section, placing the pins at a right angle to the edge.

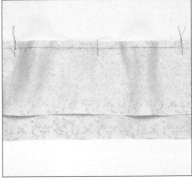

2. Pin to match the centres. Ensure there is an even amount of loose fabric on both sides of the centre pin.

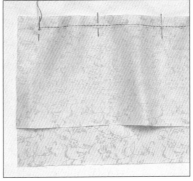

3. Distributing the fabric evenly, place the next pin midway between the centre and outer pins. Repeat on the other side. Continue in this manner until the pins are close together.

4. Pull up the machine thread, easing the fullness to fit. Ensure there are no obvious pleats. Tack the fabrics together using small close stitches. Stitch, taking care not to form pleats.

5. Trim the seam and neaten. Press carefully to steam out any rippling that may be visible on the eased side of the seam.

elastic

The following instructions are for simple techniques to attach elastic without a fabric casing.
See also; Casings with elastic on pages 55 - 57.

quick thread casing for narrow elastic

A thread casing is an easy, attractive method to create an elasticised edge for a variety of garments.
It is best worked on light to medium weight fabrics only. Use strong polyester thread to increase the
durability of the casing.

Preparation

Cut a length of elastic to fit comfortably around the body at the required position, plus seam allowances.
Stitch and finish any seams passing through the position for the elastic, leaving one seam open. Finish the
raw edge below the casing, using the desired method. It is easier to do this while the fabric is still flat.

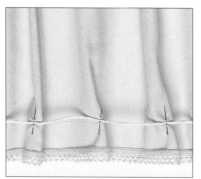

1. Mark a line on the wrong side of the fabric at the position for the elastic. Divide the line and the elastic into quarters and mark. Matching marks, pin the elastic to the fabric. Secure the ends with stitching, within the seam allowance.

2. Using a zigzag stitch fractionally wider than the elastic, stitch over the elastic without catching it. Stretch to fit flat against the fabric between the pinned positions as you stitch. Holding the fabric flat behind the presser foot is helpful.

3. The casing is now ready to have the final seam stitched to secure the ends. Ensure the ends of the elastic match, keeping the trimming aligned at the lower edge.

hints elastic

Almost all forms of elastic will eventually lose its stretch. The time frame will depend on the amount of wear and the care taken when laundering. Choose a method that allows the elastic to ride freely inside a casing if you expect to renew it.

Constant exposure to chlorine or salt water will shorten the life of general purpose elastic. Special swimwear elastic, which is resistant to the damage caused by these elements, has been developed for this purpose.

attaching underwear elastic

This one step technique provides an easy method of attaching narrow, decorative elastic to the edges of underwear. The second method is best used when applying wide elastic as a waistband.

Preparation

For both methods, cut a length of elastic to fit comfortably around the body at the required position, plus seam allowances. Stitch and finish any seams passing through the position for the elastic, leaving one seam open. Neaten the raw edge with a zigzag or overlock stitch. Divide the garment edge and the length of elastic into quarters and mark. Matching marks and with the right side of the elastic facing upwards, pin the marked edge of the elastic to the right side of the fabric. Position the elastic to overlap the fabric by 6mm (1/4").

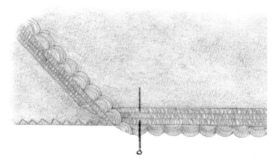

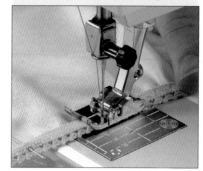

1. Using a wide, open zigzag or a tricot stitch at the widest setting, stitch along the heading of the elastic. Stretch to fit flat against the fabric between the pins.

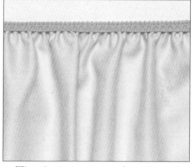

2. The elastic is now ready to have the final seam stitched to secure the ends.

TWO STEP METHOD

1. With the decorative edge of the elastic towards the garment, pin the upper edge to overlap the fabric by 6mm (1/4"). Using a medium width zigzag, stitch along the edge of the elastic. Stretch and flatten as you stitch.

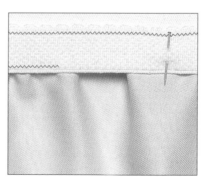

2. Wrong side. Stitch and finish the remaining garment side seam. Fold the elastic to the wrong side. Pin the lower edge to the fabric below the marked divisions. Stretch the elastic flat as you stitch.

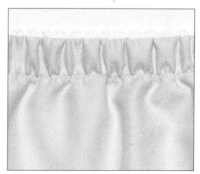

3. On the right side, the upper edge of the elastic forms a decorative finish.

elastic

eyelets

Eyelets are either small, neatened holes in the fabric, often found in embroidery designs, or tiny metal rings punched through the fabric and secured in place with a special tool. This form of eyelet is commonly found on belts, but can also be used to pass lacing through.

Use a marking pen suitable for the fabric when marking the positions of the eyelets.

hand worked eyelets

For this style of eyelet, mark a small circle on the right side of the fabric.

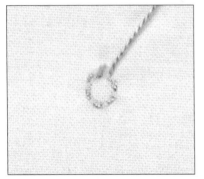

1. Leaving a short tail, work running stitch around the circle.

2. When reaching the starting point take the needle through the first stitch, splitting it.

3. Pierce the centre of the circle with an awl, separating the fabric threads.

4. Bring the thread to the front just outside the running stitch. Take the needle through the hole and emerge on the outer edge.

5. Pull the thread through. Take the needle through the hole and emerge alongside the previous stitch.

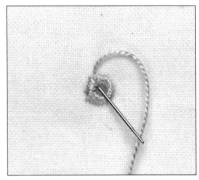

6. Continue working close overcast stitch around the circle until the edge is covered. Take the needle to the back through the hole.

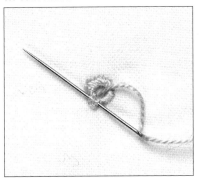

7. Secure the thread under the overcast stitches on the back.

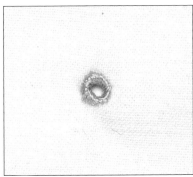

8. Carefully re-pierce the hole with the awl to ensure it is round.

metal eyelets

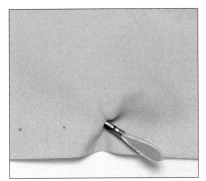

1. Pierce a large hole through the fabric at the marked position using an awl.

wrong side

2. Push the eyelet stud through the hole.

wrong side

3. Clamp the stud to the fabric using the appropriate tool.

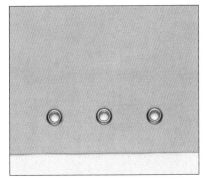

4. Finished eyelets.

hints
hand worked eyelets

Stabilise the fabric with spray starch to keep the shape of the hole even while you stitch.

The awl should pierce a hole by parting the fabric fibres, rather than breaking them.

Create a hole slightly larger than the required finished width. The stitching will fill part of the hole, making it smaller.

metal eyelets

Reinforce the area with interfacing to provide a solid background for the eyelets.

If you require a large hole, cut the fabric with a tiny cross centred on the marked point. By not removing any fabric, it will ensure the eyelet can maintain a firm grip.

Depending on the metal used, eyelets may rust if the garment is left wet for any length of time.

eyelets

facings

A facing is used to finish the raw edges of a garment. There are two basic types of facing, separate and integrated. A separate facing is cut using a pattern piece, the same shape and on the same grain as the edge it will finish. An integrated facing is an extension of the garment piece. After a facing is attached, it is turned to the wrong side and secured. It should not show on the right side. If the garment is being made from heavyweight fabric, a lighter fabric can be used for facings to reduce bulk.

See also; Faced armhole on page 31; Faced necklines on pages 101 and 102; Faced hem on page 93; Faced waistline on page 145.

combination facing

On a sleeveless garment with narrow shoulders, it is preferable to cut the armhole and neckline facings as a combined piece.

If cut separately, they create bulk at the shoulder seams.

Preparation

Staystitch the neckline and armhole edges of the front and back bodice pieces. Apply lightweight interfacing to the wrong side of the facing pieces. Ensure the end of the stitchline is marked clearly on the bodice pieces at both ends of the shoulder seam.

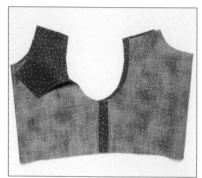

1. Pin and stitch the bodice front to the back at the sides. Neaten the seams separately and press open.

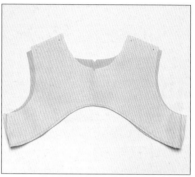

2. Repeat for the facing pieces, neatening the lower edge of the facing.

3. With right sides together, pin the facing to the bodice around the armholes and neckline. Offset the garment edges by 2mm ($^1/_{16}$") at the shoulder point. Stitch each seam to the marked point.

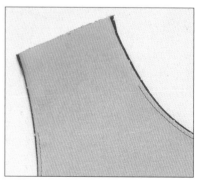

4. Trim seams and clip curves. Turn to the right side. Understitch the seams on the facing, beginning and ending as far as you can reach towards the shoulders. At the shoulders, the facing will roll slightly to the inside.

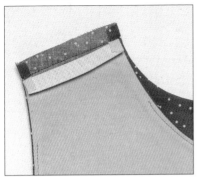

5. Press. With right sides together and keeping the facings out of the way, stitch the bodice front to the back at the shoulders.

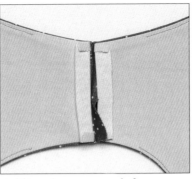

6. Trim the seams and finger press open. Push the shoulder seams through the opening and towards the back, keeping them flat.

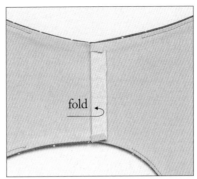

7. Trim the facing seam allowances. Fold the front facing seam allowance to the inside through the opening.

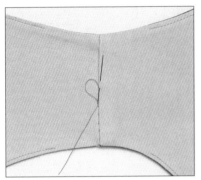

8. Fold under the back facing seam allowance. Handstitch the opening closed.

9. Press. Aligning the seams, handstitch the facing to the bodice seam at the underarm.

bias facing

Preparation. Cut the bias facing twice the finished width adding seam allowances. The length equals the seamline between the opening foldlines. Neaten the raw edges of the opening and press the foldlines.

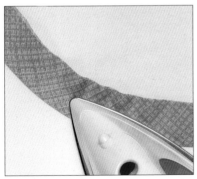

1. Fold the bias facing in half along the length. Using a steam iron, shape the folded facing, stretching the folded edge to fit the neckline curve, keeping the raw edges even.

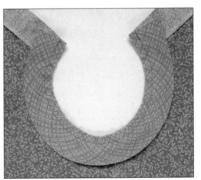

2. Fold the opening facings right sides together and pin. With right sides together and matching raw edges, pin, tack and stitch the bias facing to the neckline.

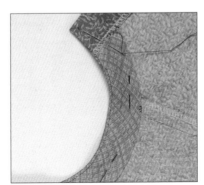

3. Trim the corners. Turn the facings to the inside and push out the corners. Understitch the neckline on the bias facing. Handstitch the binding to the shoulder seams and the facing to the binding.

facings

81

fastenings

A fastener secures the openings that allow a garment to be taken on and off easily.

Buttons, zips, hooks and eyes and snap fasteners are all simple or decorative types of fastenings.

See also; Buttons and buttonholes pages 42 - 55; Zips on pages 146 - 149.

hook and eye

This fastener should be used on opening edges that butt together.

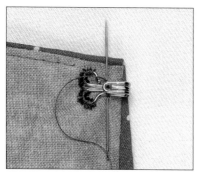

1. Position the hook on the inside of one edge. Whip around each hole. Bring the thread to the front near the shaft. Whip over the shaft to hold the hook flat against the fabric.

2. Position the eye in the corresponding position on the opposite edge. Whip around each hole then stitch over the arms of the eye to hold flat against the fabric.

hook and bar

This fastening type is used for added strength on waistbands.

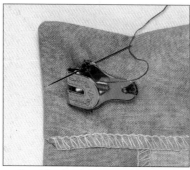

1. Sew the hook into position on the wrong side of the overlap, ensuring the stitching doesn't show on the right side.

2. Sew the bar into position on the opposite edge of the opening to correspond.

hook and thread loop

An alternative to the metal eye is a blanket stitched loop or bar.

METHOD ONE

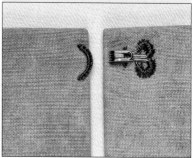

Butted closure. Sew the hook into position on one edge of the opening. Mark upper and lower placement of thread loop to correspond on the other edge of the opening. Stitch the loop following the instructions on page 50.

METHOD TWO

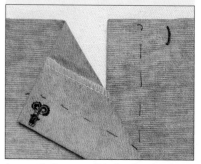

Lapped closure. Stitch the hook as before on the wrong side of the overlap. Mark and stitch the thread loop at the corresponding position.

hook and loop tape

The tape must be attached to an overlapped opening. Generally, the hooked nap tape is sewn to the underside of the overlap, allowing it to be pressed into the fuzzy nap to make the connection more secure.

With the two tapes pressed together, measure and cut the length needed to secure the opening. Pull the tapes apart and stitch the fuzzy tape into position on the underlap by stitching around the edge. Place the overlap in position on the tape and mark the placement of the hook tape. Stitch the hook tape in place as before.

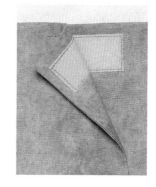

snap fasteners sew on fasteners

These small fasteners are used on closures with very little strain and come in a range of sizes to suit the application. They are made from metal or clear plastic and consist of a ball section that fits into a socket section.

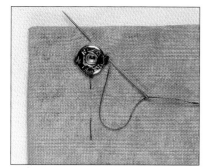

1. Position the socket section on the underlap, 6mm (¼") from the upper edge. Stitch in place with overcast stitches into each hole.

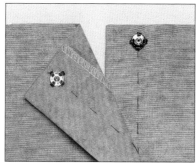

2. Lap the closure and mark the position of the ball section on the overlap. Attach this section in a similar manner, carrying the thread between the layers of fabric.

Lingerie strap. Designed to hold bra straps in place, these can be purchased ready made or constructed using narrow ribbon. Construct the strap as shown and stitch in place on the shoulder seam.

popper stud

A no-sew, stronger grip version of the snap fastener is the popper stud. This is useful for areas of greater strain, especially on denim or leather and the inside leg openings of baby wear. A special assembly tool is required and is often supplied with the popper stud kit.

1. Position and attach the upper section of the stud on the wrong side of the overlap, following the manufacturer's instructions.

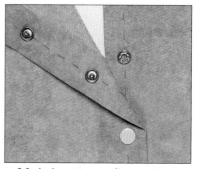

2. Mark the corresponding position on the underlap and repeat for the stud socket.

gathering

Gathering is a technique that draws in a greater amount of fabric to fit a smaller area. Gathers are most often used at waistlines, sleeve cuffs, below yokes and for ruffles and frills. For gentle gathering, the fabric allowance should be twice the finished width and for full gathers, three times the width or more, depending on the weight of the fabric. Gathers drape best on the straight grain. When gathering extended lengths, divide the area into smaller sections to make the gathering more manageable and to avoid broken threads. Leaving long threads, stop and start the gathering rows at each section. Refer to your machine manual for correct stitch length and tension for gathering.

attaching a gathered edge

Preparation

Gathering is usually done after all construction seams in the gathered fabric and the garment piece have been stitched, finished and pressed. On some pieces, such as the head of a sleeve, the gathering rows are easier to stitch while the piece is flat.

To ensure the gathering is even, divide the edge of the gathering fabric and the edge of the garment into quarters. Mark the points on the edge of the fabric. When attaching a gathered skirt to the lower edge of a bodice, these marks will be the centre front, back and the side seams.

1. Stitching on the right side, work two rows of gathering 4mm ($^3/_{16}$") from the stitchline on either side.

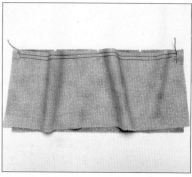

2. With right sides together and matching marks, pin the gathered fabric to the garment edge. Anchor the bobbin threads at one end by winding around a pin in a figure 8.

3. Pull on the free bobbin thread tails while gliding the fabric along the threads into even gathers. When the first section fits the garment edge, tie the bobbin threads together to secure.

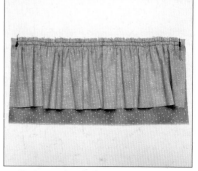

4. Release the bobbin threads at the other end and gather the second section in the same manner. Tie the thread tails together. Even out the gathers along the entire length and pin at regular intervals.

... continued

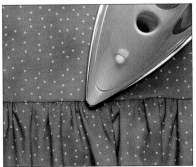

joining gathered edges

5. Re-adjust the machine stitch length and tension for normal sewing. Stitch the gathered fabric to the garment, placing the stitching halfway between the gathering rows.

6. Trim and neaten the seam. Pull out the gathering threads. Press the seam towards the flat fabric, using only the tip of the iron.

This type of seam is not very strong and the stitching may break under strain. It requires a 'stay' to reinforce the seam, allowing it to retain its original shape. Stays can be created from any narrow strip with finished edges and a straight grain such as cotton tape, ribbon or woven seam binding.

Preparation

Cut a piece of stay tape to match the length of the finished seam. Transfer any pattern markings to the tape. Stitch gathering rows on the edge of both pieces of fabric following step 1 of the previous instructions.

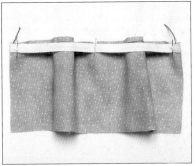

1. With the markings matching, centre the tape along the stitchline on the wrong side of the first fabric piece. Matching markings, pin to the fabric.

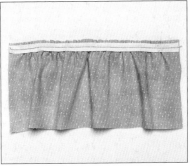

2. Gather the fabric to match the tape, Baste the tape in place along the centre.

3. With right sides together and matching raw edges and markings, pin the ungathered edge of the second fabric piece to the first. Gather to fit the tape.

4. Stitch, following the previous stitching. Trim and neaten the seam.

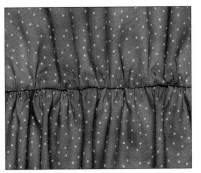

5. Separate the two pieces and finger press the seam to sit facing upwards. It should not require pressing.

gathering

85

handstitching

The sewing machine can be the home sewer's best friend, but there are still many instances where neat handstitching is required to give a superior finish to a garment.

Select a needle suitable for the thread and the particular stitch you are using. A fine needle with a small eye is best. Choose a short needle for single stitches like hemming and a longer needle for taking multiple stitches at one time such as running stitch.

The thread should be strong and suited to the purpose and the fibre content of the fabric. Use matching thread for permanent stitching, as it should be invisible. Twisting and knotting can be a problem but generally, if you use good quality thread this will be kept to a minimum. Using short lengths and trying not to twist the needle excessively, will also help. When twisting does occur, let the needle hang freely on the thread, allowing it to untwist.

knotting a thread

Use a knot to secure the beginning of temporary stitching as it can be removed easily by pulling on the knot.

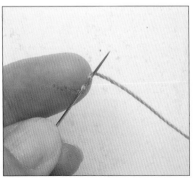

1. Hold a thread tail under the needle with your left index finger. Depending on the size of the knot, wrap the thread around the needle 2 or 3 times.

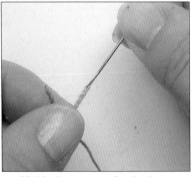

2. Hold the wraps firmly between thumb and index finger. Slowly pull the needle through.

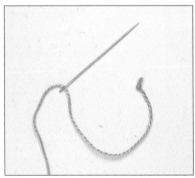

3. Continue pulling until the thread resists. Tug the knot to lock it in position. Trim the tail close to the knot.

back stitch

Although back stitch isn't usually used to construct a whole garment now, it is still one of the most versatile of the handstitches. Back stitch is useful to repair seams where it isn't practical to use a sewing machine. A few back stitches worked over each other is still the most efficient way to begin and end a line of handstitching without using knots.

Neat back stitches should look like machine stitching on the right side. Secure the thread on the wrong side, close to where you intend to begin stitching.

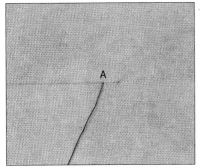

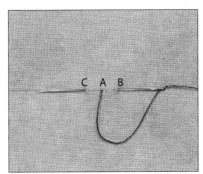

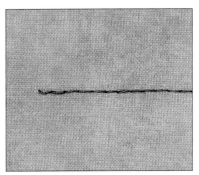

1. Bring the thread to the front at A, a short distance ahead of where the stitching should begin.

2. Take the needle from B to C. C to A should be the same distance as A to B.

3. Pull the thread through. Continue stitching in the same manner. To end off, take the thread to the back through the last hole of the previous stitch.

blanket stitch

Traditionally used in embroidery, this stitch can also be used to neaten fabric edges or decoratively secure a narrow folded hem during garment construction.

Another use is forming thread loops, as shown on pages 36 and 50.

Work from left to right with the edge of the fabric and the tip of the needle towards you.

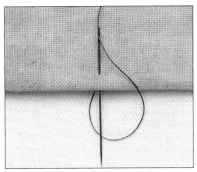

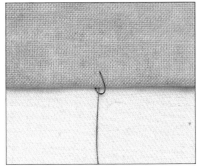

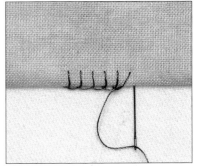

1. Secure the thread and bring it to the front below the edge of the fabric. With the thread under the tip, take the needle through the fabric and out under the edge.

2. Pull the thread through and settle the loop on the fabric edge.

3. Continue in this manner, keeping the depth of the stitches even and at right angles to the edge. To end off, take the thread to the back and secure.

handstitching

ladder stitch

An opening is often left in a seam to allow sections of a garment to be turned through to the right side. Ladder stitch is used to close the opening with concealed stitching.

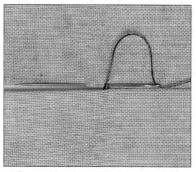 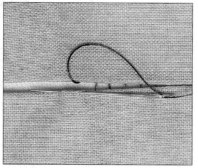 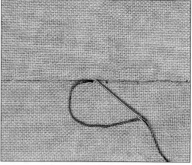

1. Secure the thread in the seam. Bring to the front on the fold on one side of the opening. Beginning level with the emerging thread, take a small stitch through the fold on the opposite side of the opening.

2. Pull the thread through without closing the opening. Take a few more stitches in a similar manner, alternating between the edges of the opening.

3. Pull on the thread gently to bring the edges of the opening together. Continue stitching from side to side, closing the opening after every few stitches. Secure the thread in the seam on the back.

overcast stitch

This stitch is used to neaten a raw edge by hand. Bring the needle through the fabric 3mm (1/8") from the edge. Pull the thread through. Take another stitch 6mm (1/4") from the first. Continue along the edge in the same manner.

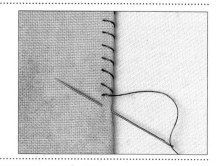

running stitch

This stitch can be both functional and decorative. It is stitched in a similar manner to tacking, but the stitches are quite small and evenly spaced. Take the needle in and out of the fabric, picking up a number of stitches before pulling the thread through. The stitches should be approximately 3mm (1/8") long on both sides of the fabric.

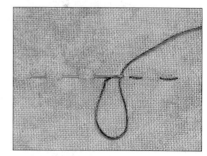

hemming stitches

A hem should be secured with neat, evenly spaced stitches that are almost invisible on the right side. Keep each stitch slightly loose. Pulling the thread too tight will disturb the surface of the fabric on the right side, making the hem more noticeable.

hemstitch

This stitch is used to secure a hem with a flat neatened edge, to flat fabric. Begin at a seam if possible, securing the thread on the edge of the hem.

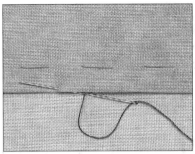

1. Pick up one or two fabric threads on the garment and pull the thread through. Take the needle through the hem edge, level with the emerging thread 6mm (¹/₄") from the first stitch.

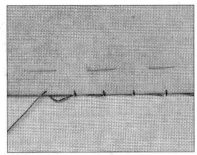

2. Pull the thread through, leaving the stitch slightly loose. Continue in the same manner.

herringbone stitch

Most hemming stitches will break if the hem stretches out of shape. To minimise this, herringbone stitch can be used to secure hems or facings, where some allowance for movement between the fabrics is necessary. This stitch stretches with the fabric, which also makes it suitable for hems on knits. Work from left to right.

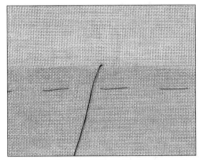

1. Secure the thread and bring it to the front on the edge of the hem.

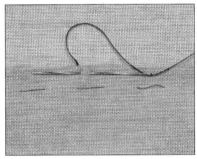

2. Take a small horizontal stitch close to the edge of the hem.

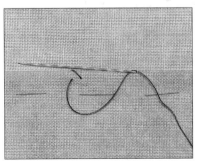

3. With the thread below the needle, take the same stitch 6mm (¹/₄") to the right, picking up a few fabric threads level with the edge of the hem.

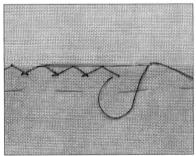

4. Repeat step 2, 6mm (¹/₄") to the right of the previous stitch. Continue in the same manner.

blind herringbone stitch

This is worked between the two fabric layers and is invisible when the hem is pressed in position. It is worked in a similar manner to herringbone stitch, placing the stitches on the inside of the hem edge. The stitches must be positioned at the same level on the garment as they are on the hem, to ensure the hem will remain at the measured depth.

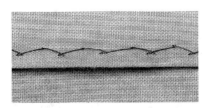

slipstitch

This is the neatest method of securing a folded edge to flat fabric as the stitches are concealed in the fold on the wrong side and are almost invisible on the right side. Begin at a seam if possible.

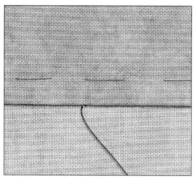

1. Secure the thread with back stitches in the fold of the hem.

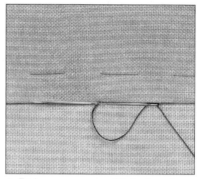

2. Pick up one or two fabric threads on the garment, level with the emerging thread on the hem.

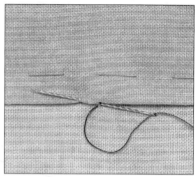

3. Pull the thread through. Slide the needle through the folded edge and emerge 6mm (1/4") away.

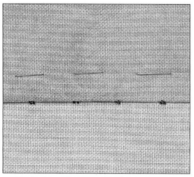

4. Pull the thread through, leaving the stitch slightly loose. Continue in the same manner.

tacking
basic tacking

Tacking is useful to hold surfaces together in the correct position until you can machine

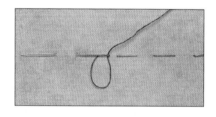

stitch them. Avoid securing the ends as this will make it difficult to remove the thread when it is no longer required. Take the needle in and out of the fabric, making large stitches roughly the same length on both sides of the fabric. Use light coloured thread to avoid marks.

diagonal tacking

When large areas need to be tacked quickly, work diagonal stitches in rows or as a filling. This is useful for holding pleats or non-fusible interfacing until they are permanently secured.

Bring the thread to the front on the lower left. Leaving a long diagonal stitch on the surface, take a large horizontal stitch through the fabric.

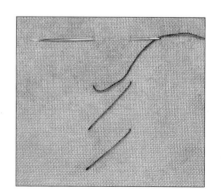

hems

A hem is a finished turning on the lower edge of any section of a garment. Choosing a hemming method will largely depend on the style of the garment and the fabric being used. For a professional result, a hem should always hang evenly and straight, without puckering around the stitching or the folded edge. Unless it is meant to be decorative, a hem should be inconspicuous. A simple turned back, handstitched hem is the method most commonly used, but a hem can also be faced or bound.

Preparation. Accurate marking is the first step to achieve the best results. For straight skirts, dresses, tops and pants, lay the garment on a flat surface and mark the hem allowance on the right side with pins. Fold under the hem along the pinned line and pin in place. Try the garment on and repin any adjustments. Lay the garment out flat again and trim off any excess fabric if necessary. Secure in place using one of the following methods.

neatened edge

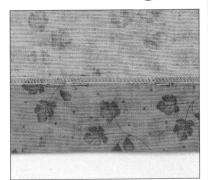

Finish the raw edge with a zigzag or overlock stitch. Secure the hem using your chosen method and press.

folded edge

Press under 6mm (¼") on the raw edge. Secure the hem using your chosen method and press.

curved edge

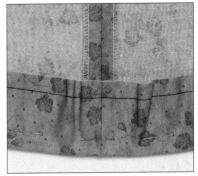

1. Work a row of machine easing 1cm (³/₈") from the raw edge. Press under with the stitching on the fold. Unfold.

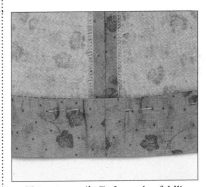

2. Trim 6mm (¼") from the foldline. Refold along the stitchline. Ease the folded hem to fit the flat fabric and pin in place. Hemstitch to secure. Press.

hems

using bias binding

Bias binding is an effective hem finish for flared skirts as the bias adjusts to fit the curves without rippling. It is also a useful method for hemming thick fabrics. Use a narrow width of bias binding, in a matching colour.

1. Unfold one edge of the binding. With right sides together, stitch the unfolded edge of the binding to the hem.

2. Press the binding away from the hem. Pin the hem in place and hemstitch or slipstitch to secure. Press.

machine stitched hems
blind hem

Use the blind hem presser foot and set the machine to a blind hemming stitch with the single zigzag stitches approximately 1cm (³⁄₈") apart. The width setting should be 2.5 or 3.

1. Neaten or fold the raw edge. Place the garment with the right side facing up and fold back to reveal 4mm (³⁄₁₆") of hem edge. Pin and tack the layers together near the fold.

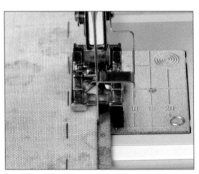

2. Keeping the centre bar on the foot aligned with the fold, stitch the hem catching a few threads of the garment with the zigzag stitches.

rolled hem

Rolled hems should be stitched starting at a raw edge at one side. Use the rolled hem presser foot and set the machine to a mid-length straight stitch.

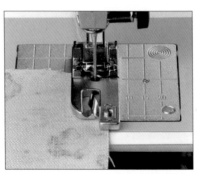

1. Lower the needle into the fabric edge. Work a few stitches, turning the flywheel by hand. Hold the threads at the back. Roll the fabric edge into the tunnel of the presser foot.

2. Holding the threads, begin sewing, guiding 6 - 8mm (¹⁄₄" - ⁵⁄₁₆") of the fabric folded in front of the foot. The depth of the fold will determine the finished width of the hem.

faced hem

also called false hem

A faced hem is not only useful to gain extra length in a garment, it can also be invaluable to achieve a flat hem on a curved edge or to reduce bulk on a garment made from thick fabric.

Preparation. Stitch and finish all seams in the garment and facing.

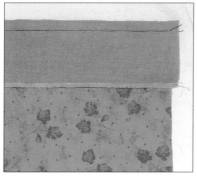

1. With right sides together and matching seams and centres, pin the facing to the garment edge. Stitch.

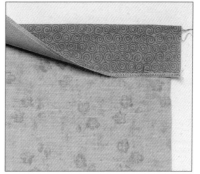

2. Trim the seam. Press to one side and fold the facing to the inside, slightly rolling the seam. Secure the hem by hand or machine.

hems - securing a faced corner

There are two ways to finish a hem where it meets a faced opening. The first will allow the hem to be adjusted if required. The second is permanently fixed. The instructions show a seam attaching the facing, but the method is the same if using an integrated facing.

METHOD ONE

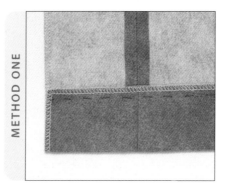

1. Pressing any seams open, pin the hem in position and tack. Secure the hem by hand or machine.

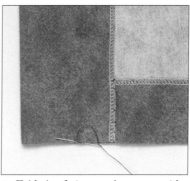

2. Fold the facing to the wrong side, aligning the lower edges. Handstitch the lower edge closed and the facing to the hem.

METHOD TWO

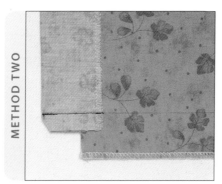

1. Mark the hem foldline. With right sides facing, stitch across the lower edge of the facing just below the line. Trim the lower edge and clip the corner as shown.

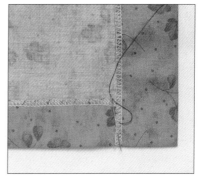

2. Turn through to the right side. Handstitch the hem and the facing edge to the hem.

interfacing

attaching non-fusible interfacing

Non-fusible interfacings are held in place on the wrong side of the corresponding pattern piece with tacking. Any tacking should remain until after the garment pieces are joined and pressed. Ensure the tacking is clearly visible from the right side as you will not be able to access it from the inside. Cut out the garment piece and corresponding interfacing piece according to the pattern.

heavyweight non-fusible interfacing

Heavyweight interfacings add bulk and are only attached up to the stitchline, not into the seam allowances. Cut away the seam allowances and the hems on all edges of the interfacing piece.

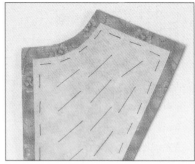

1. Aligning the edges with the stitch-line, pin the interfacing onto the wrong side of the fabric. Tack just inside the edge. For large areas, work diagonal tacking in the centre, to keep the interfacing flat.

2. Work herringbone stitch around the edge of the interfacing, stitching through the seam allowance and catching the interfacing only.

3. With right sides facing, pin the garment pieces together. Stitch along the edge of the interfacing, catching the herringbone stitches in the seam.

lightweight non-fusible interfacing

As lightweight interfacings do not add a great amount of bulk to a seam, the interfacing is cut the same as the pattern piece.

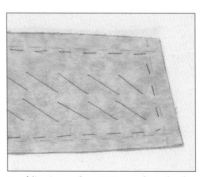

1. Aligning edges, pin and tack the interfacing to the wrong side of the garment piece in the same manner as above.

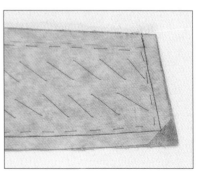

2. With right sides facing, pin the garment pieces together. Stitch along the stitchline. Trim the interfacing at any corners.

applying fusible interfacing

Fusible interfacing comes in many weights. It has a heat-activated adhesive coating on one surface which bonds to the fabric. The adhesive side is the wrong side. Always test the interfacing on a scrap of the fabric first. Unsuitable fabrics include velvet and some textured fabrics like seersucker. Cut out the garment and corresponding interfacing pieces according to the pattern, ensuring the adhesive side of each interfacing piece will face the wrong side of the fabric. Transfer any pattern markings to the right side of the interfacing.

heavyweight fusible interfacings

These add bulk to the seam allowances. As the interfacing is fused to the fabric, only a small amount of the seam allowance remains and is stitched into the seam.

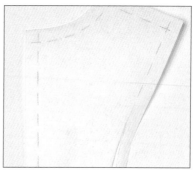

1. Trim the seam allowances just outside the stitchline.

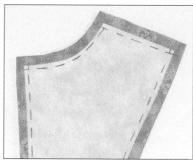

2. Aligning stitchlines, fuse the interfacing to the wrong side of the garment piece.

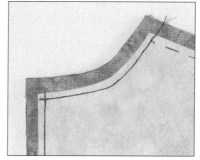

3. With right sides facing, pin the garment pieces together. Stitch along the stitchline.

lightweight fusible interfacing

This does not add much bulk at all, so removing the seam allowance is unnecessary. It will be trimmed back, along with the fabric allowance, after the seam is stitched.

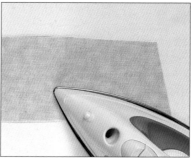

1. Aligning edges, fuse the interfacing to the wrong side of the garment piece.

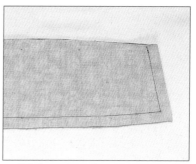

2. With right sides facing, pin the garment pieces together. Stitch along the stitchline.

linings

A lining is applied to the inside of a garment to add to its structure and conceal the seams. It is most often made from a slippery fabric to allow the garment to slide easily over other clothing.

A lining is usually secured on all edges within the garment, however, a free hanging lining floats inside the garment, suspended from the shoulders or a waistband.

Half linings can also be applied to the upper half of a skirt or trousers, to provide support at the front or to stop the main fabric from 'bagging' at the back when seated.

If a garment is finished with a secured lining, the seams need not be neatened as they won't be subjected to abrasion when concealed by the lining.

Darts and seams should always be in the same place on the lining as they are on the outer layer. Some exceptions are small pleats and easing that are often part of the lining to allow for movement when the garment is worn. Construction details such as darts should always be pressed in the same direction on the lining as they are on the outer layer.

An interlining is a separate layer of fabric or interfacing, which is applied to the wrong side of the main fabric. Both layers are basted together around the outer edge and treated as one layer during construction.

edge-to-edge lining

This type of lining is a mirror image of the outer layer, attached along the outer edges. Methods for attaching this style of lining will vary depending on the style of garment. Refer to your pattern instructions.

Preparation. Cut out the main garment pieces and then cut a copy of each piece to use as a lining.

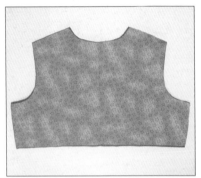

1. Layer each garment and lining piece to ensure they match. Trim any edges if necessary.

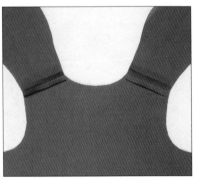

2. Construct all internal seams leaving an opening at each side seam. Repeat for the lining.

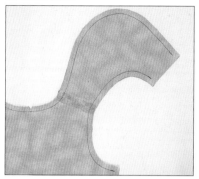

3. With right sides together and matching raw edges, seams and markings, pin and stitch the garment to the lining around the outer edges. Begin and end at the marked points.

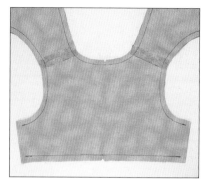

4. Repeat on the lower edge of the back.

free hanging

A free hanging lining is a duplicate layer of the outer fabric section that 'floats' inside a garment. It is secured on the inside of the upper edge.
The lower edges are hemmed separately allowing the lining to move independently.
These are commonly used on skirts, dresses and long coats.

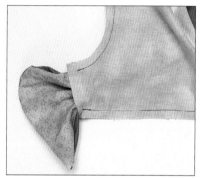

5. Trim the seams and clip or notch the curves. Turn the garment to the right side through a side seam opening.

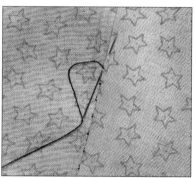

6. With right sides together, stitch and finish the garment side seams in the same manner as the facing shoulder seams, steps 5 - 8 on page 81.

1. Construct the outer and lining layers of the garment separately. If necessary, insert a zip into the outer layer.

7. Roll the seams to the outer edge and press.

hint
edge-to-edge lining

Making the handstitching invisible will allow the garment to become fully reversible.

2. Turn the outer layer to the right side. With wrong sides together, slide the lining into the outer layer. Matching centres, seams and markings, tack the layers together on the upper edge.

linings

... *continued*

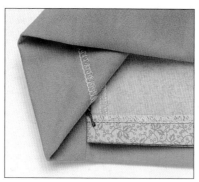

3. Fold under the opening on the lining to align with the stitching. Pin and handstitch in place. Attach the waistband.

4. Fold and secure a hem on the garment. Press. Repeat for the lining leaving it 3cm (1 ¼") shorter than the garment. At each side seam, attach the lining to the garment with a 2cm (³/₄") thread loop.

faced lining

A lining is often formed with a facing at the leading edge to ensure it remains hidden. The facing is made from the same fabric as the outer layer.

Preparation

On the pattern piece for the outer layer, mark a line a short distance away from the opening edge. Cut through the line and make new pattern pieces, adding at least 1cm (³/₈") on each side of the cut edge for the seam allowance.

facing

pattern piece

lining

Cut the pieces for the outer layer using the original pattern piece. Cut the facings and the lining using the new pattern pieces.

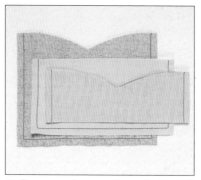

1. Construct the outer layer, facing and lining separately.

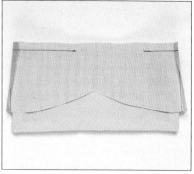

2. Trim the seams and press open. With right sides together and leaving an opening, pin and stitch the lower edge of the facing to the upper edge of the lining.

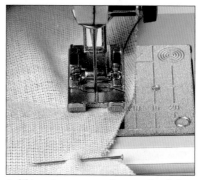

3. Trim the seam and press the facing away from the lining. With right sides together and matching seams, pin and stitch the lining to the outer layer.

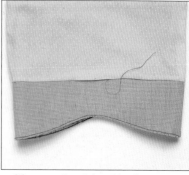

4. Turn to the right side through the opening. Roll the seam to the edge. Topstitch or edgestitch to secure the facing. Handstitch the opening closed.

necklines

Necklines can be finished with binding, a facing or feature a collar.
See also; attaching collars on page 66 - 68; combination facing on page 80.

bound neckline

When using a pattern where the neckline is not specifically designed for a bound edge, it is necessary to trim away the seam allowance. See pages 39 and 40 for more information on bound edges. The following instructions are for attaching a single binding, but would work just as well for a double binding.

Preparation

Prepare the neckline by stitching and pressing the shoulder seams. Attach or construct any facings or linings along the opening edge. Attach any decorative elements such as piping, lace, keyholes or front button tabs. Mark the centre front and back on the neckline.

overlapping

With this technique, the binding overlaps at the back buttonband, creating bulk at that point. This method is suitable for light to medium-weight fabrics only. Prepare the garment as described above and baste the facing or lining in place at the neckline.

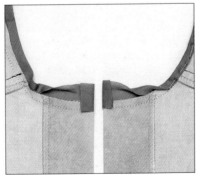

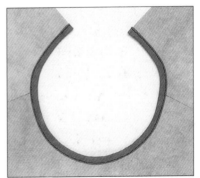

1. With right sides together and matching raw edges along the neckline, pin the binding in place, allowing a seam allowance to extend at both ends. Stitch.

2. Fold in the seam allowance at the ends of the binding. Fold the binding to the wrong side, enclosing the seam allowance. Pin and tack the fold to just cover the previous stitchline.

3. Machine stitch on the right side along the edge of the binding. Press.

butted binding

With this technique the ends of the binding butt together at the centre back, allowing just the extensions on the button closure to overlap. It is suitable for heavier weight fabrics and for necklines finished with lace or fabric frills.

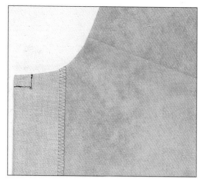

1. Fold the back bodice and facing, right sides together at the upper edge. Stitch down from the centre back neckline, for the width of the binding. Pivot and stitch to the folded edge.

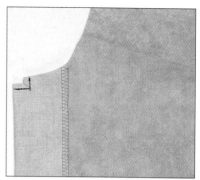

2. Trim the seam, leaving a small seam allowance. Clip the inner corner.

hint
ready made binding

Using ready made binding, unfold one edge and use this edge to attach the binding, following the foldline as a guide for the stitching

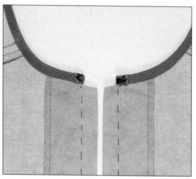

3. Turn through to the right side. Pushing out the corner, tack the facing in place. Attach the binding following steps 1 - 3 on the previous page. Stitch a hook and loop at the ends of the binding.

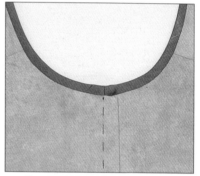

4. Press the neckline gently. By eliminating the overlapped binding, the bulk at the back neckline is reduced and a flatter finish is achieved.

faced necklines

Almost any shape, from a simple round neck to more complicated scallops and keyholes, can be built into the neckline using this method.

Neckline facings are usually separate pieces of the garment fabric, but may be cut from lighter fabric to reduce bulk. They are cut on the same grain and mirror the shape at the neckline and openings of the garment pieces.

Although the pattern you have chosen may have a different neckline shape to the one shown, all facings are constructed in a similar manner.

See page 80 for a combined neck and armhole facing.

See page 66 and 67 for using a facing to attach a collar.

Preparation

Apply interfacing to the wrong side of the facing pieces.

Staystitch just inside the neckline seam allowance of the garment pieces.

simple faced neckline

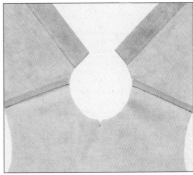

1. With right sides together, pin, stitch and finish the bodice seams. Construct any openings.

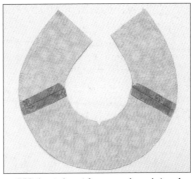

2. With right sides together, join the facing pieces at the shoulders. Trim the seams and press open. Neaten the outer raw edge.

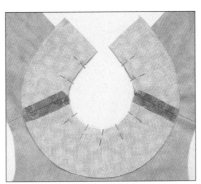

3. With right sides together and matching seams, centres and raw edges along the neckline, pin the facing in place.

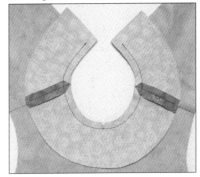

4. With the facing uppermost and beginning at the centre, stitch around one half of the neckline at a time.

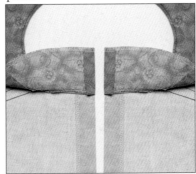

5. Trim the seam and grade if necessary. Clip the curve. Press the facing and seam away from the garment. Understitch the seam on the facing. Press under the allowance on both sides of the opening.

6. Fold the facing to the wrong side and press. Handstitch the edge of the facing to the opening edge and shoulder seams.

necklines

101

combined neck and front opening

For this type of facing, the back neck and front opening facings become a continuous piece. The following instructions show a front opening, but the opening could alternatively be at the back.

Preparation

Apply interfacing to the wrong side of the facing pieces. Staystitch just inside the neckline seam allowance of the garment pieces.

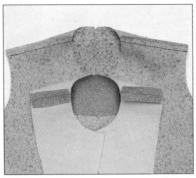

1. Prepare the garment and facing following steps 1 and 2 on page 101.

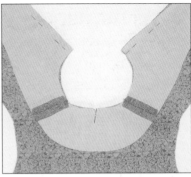

2. With right sides together and matching raw edges, seams and centres, pin and tack the facing to the neckline and opening.

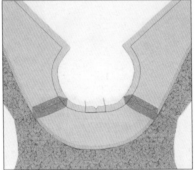

3. Beginning at the centre, stitch around the neckline and down one side of the opening. With the garment uppermost, return to the centre and complete the seam.

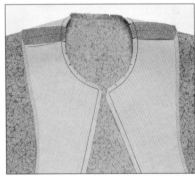

4. Trim the seam and grade if necessary. Clip the curves and corners.

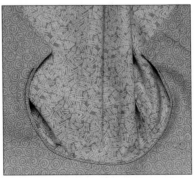

5. Press the facing and seam away from the garment. Understitch the seam on the facing, beginning and ending close to the corner point. Repeat for the opening.

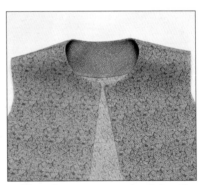

6. Turn the garment to the right side. Handstitch the edge of the facing to the garment shoulder seams.

placket opening

This simple placket is a neat way to create a partial neckline opening. The following instructions allow for a 2.5cm (1") wide placket, suitable for adult garments. Ensure the opening is deep enough to allow the garment to slip over the head.

Preparation. Fold the front bodice in half and finger press the centre front. Measure and mark a line from the neckline along the fold, 1cm (3/8") shorter than the opening. Cut a 6mm (1/4") wide slit on the marked line. Stitch and finish the shoulder seams. Prepare the garment and neckline following step 2 on page 101. Cut two placket pieces, each 7cm (2 3/4") wide and 2cm (3/4") longer than the finished opening. Apply interfacing to half the width of each piece, ensuring you have a left and a right piece.

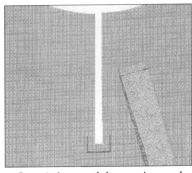

1. Staystitch around the opening on the front and clip diagonally into the corners. Fold the placket pieces in half, right sides together. Stitch across the upper end.

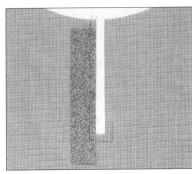

2. Trim the seam and clip the corner. Turn to the right side. With right sides together, align the finished placket end with the neck stitchline. Matching raw edges at the opening, pin and stitch along the length, finishing at the base of the placket opening.

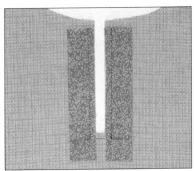

3. Attach the remaining placket piece in the same manner to the opposite side of the opening. Mark the stitchline across the lower edge.

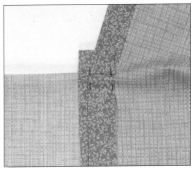

4. Rotate the folded edge of the upper placket counter-clockwise to match the opposite stitchline.

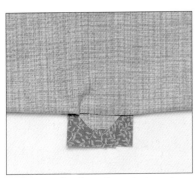

5. Repeat for the other placket piece. Fold the garment to expose the ends of the placket. Stitch through all layers.

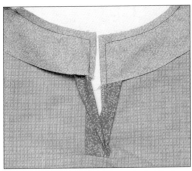

6. Neaten the seams. Attach the facing, keeping the upper edges of the placket out of the way, stitching along the previous opening stitch lines.

7. Trim and clip the seam and corners. Press towards the facing and understitch. Press and attach the facing to the shoulder seams.

piping

Piping is a narrow fabric trim inserted into a seam to strengthen and define an edge. It can be both flat or corded, with the fabric cut on the straight grain or the bias. See pages 36 - 38 for cutting and joining lengths of bias fabric.

The width or thickness of the piping should always be in keeping with the scale of the project - extra fine for babies' and children's wear, up to the heavy corded piping used in upholstery and soft furnishing items.

Flat piping consists of a fabric strip folded in half along the length and pressed flat. The width of the strip is calculated as twice the width of the finished piping, plus twice the required seam allowance. It is inserted into a seam in the same manner as corded piping.

Corded piping is constructed by sewing a length of twisted cotton cord inside the tunnel of a strip of bias cut fabric.

A zipper foot is useful for stitching close to the cord.

To determine the width of the fabric strip, sandwich a piece of piping in the looped end of a tape measure. Wrap the tape measure around the cord until it extends by the seam allowance you will be using. The length of the piping will equal the measurement 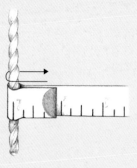 along the edge to be piped, adding extra to go around corners and to join the piping into a continuous length if necessary.

corded piping

1. Cut and construct a continuous length of bias fabric following the steps on page 36. Lay the cord along the centre of the strip on the wrong side.

2. With wrong sides together and matching raw edges, fold the fabric over the cord. Stitch as close to the cord as possible using a zipper foot.

hint piping

If the depth of the piping seam allowance is different to the seam allowance you are using, match the stitchline on the piping to the stitchline on the garment piece.

attaching piping to a straight edge

1. Matching stitchlines, pin the piping to the right side of the garment piece. Stitch along the piping stitchline.

2. Matching raw edges, pin the remaining fabric piece over the piping. Tack the layers together within the seam allowance. Stitch between the previous stitchline and the corded edge of the piping.

3. Trim the seam. Turn to the right side. To place the piping on the edge, understitch the seam on the back. Press carefully, taking care not to crush the piping.

attaching piping to a curved edge

Preparation. Clip the piping seam allowance at even intervals - the tighter the curve, the closer the clips.

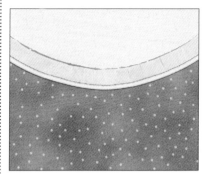

1. Concave curve. Matching stitchlines, pin and tack the piping to the right side of the garment, shaping it to fit the curve. Stitch along the piping stitchline.

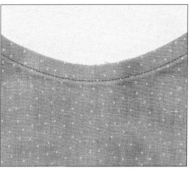

2. Matching raw edges, pin the remaining fabric piece over the piping. Tack the layers together within the seam allowance. Stitch between the previous stitchline and the corded edge of the piping.

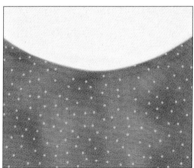

3. Trim the seam and clip the curve. Understitch the seam if needed. Fold with the piping on the outer edge and press carefully. Take care not to crush the piping.

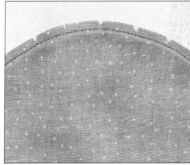

4. Convex curve. The instructions are the same as concave curves except that the curve is notched before being turned to the right side as in step 3.

hint piping

To eliminate excess bulk in seams that cross the ends of a piping strip, remove the cord from the end of the piping to the stitchline. Pinch the end of the cord between your fingers and carefully ease the fabric back until the desired length of cord is exposed. Trim off the cord and pull the fabric back into position. Without being secured at the ends, the cord will 'float' within the tube.

piping

piping a sharp corner

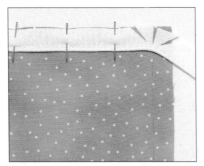

1. Pin the piping in place. Clip the piping seam allowance to the stitching at the corner point. Clip diagonally on either side.

2. Turn the piping around the corner, allowing the clipped seam allowance to open. Continue to pin the piping. Stitch along the piping stitchline.

continuous piping

When piping is required around a complete shape such as a cushion or sleeve band, join the piping at the point where the ends meet, usually in an inconspicuous spot or aligned with a seam.

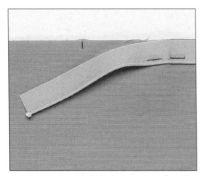

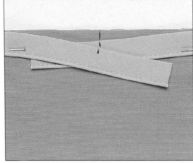

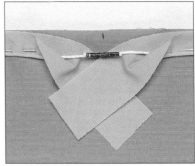

1. Method one. Mark a point for the join on the edge of the fabric. Begin pinning the piping to the fabric, allowing 3cm (1¼") to extend past the mark.

2. Pin piping around the shape, finishing with the end extending past the starting point. Mark the edge of both piping ends level with the mark on the fabric.

3. Unpick the piping stitching for 7.5cm (3") at the ends. Measure and cut off excess cord at the marked point allowing 1cm (³⁄₈") to overlap. Bind and secure.

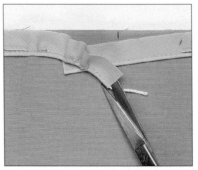

4. Trim excess piping fabric and stitch the join, following the instructions on page 38. Reposition the cord and replace the stitching. Re-pin the piping to the fabric edge.

5. Method two. Mark the join on the fabric stitchline. Pin the piping to the fabric, allowing 3cm (1 ¼") to extend past the mark. Carefully pull the cord out and trim level with the mark.

6. Overlap the piping seam allowances at the mark, curving the ends into the seam and pin. Stitch the piping to the fabric. Trim the ends.

plackets

A placket is a functional detail neatening a partial opening in a garment.

hemmed

Preparation. At the required position, mark a line 1cm (³/₈") longer than the finished length of the opening, at a right angle to the raw edge. Cut along the line.

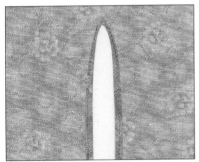

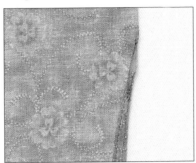

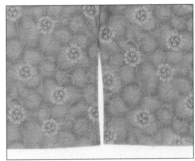

1. Fold and stitch narrow double folded hems on both sides of the opening, tapering at the cut point.

2. With right sides together, align the hemmed edges. Stitch a tiny dart.

3. Press the dart to one side at the end of the placket.

faced

Preparation. At the required position, mark a line slightly shorter than the finished length of the opening, at a right angle to the raw edge. Cut a rectangle for the facing in proportion to the size of the opening. Mark the same line, centred on the lower edge of the facing. Neaten the outer edge of the facing. Cut along the line on the garment and the facing.

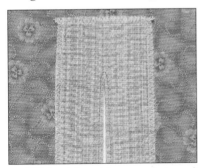

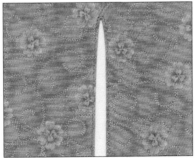

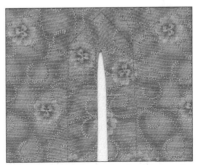

1. With right sides together and matching lines, pin the facing in place. Stitch along both sides of the opening, beginning and ending 4mm (³/₁₆") from the edge and tapering to a point above the cut.

2. Clip the seam at the cut end. Press the seam and facing away from the opening. Fold the facing to the inside. Edgestitch around the opening. Hand-stitch the outer edges of the facing to secure. Press.

2a. Alternatively, tack the facing in position and topstitch from the right side, placing the stitching an even distance from the opening.

plackets

lapped placket

This type of placket provides a narrow binding for the raw edge of the opening. The number of layers required makes it unsuitable for thick fabrics.

Preparation

For method two, crease a fold at a right angle to the raw edge, for a short distance at the position for the opening on the garment. Mark a line on the fold for the required distance from the edge.

Cut the width of the strip for the placket, twice the finished width plus two seam allowances and double the length of the opening.

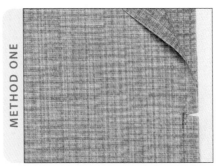

1. Seamed opening. Stitch the seam, leaving an opening for the desired length of the placket. Clip the seam allowance, angling the cut to the end of the stitching.

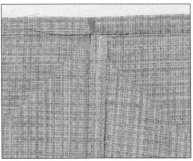

2. Trim and neaten the stitched seam to the clipped point. Press to one side. Spread the opening. With right sides together, pin the placket strip along the opening. Stitch, just catching the neatened end of the seam. Finish the placket, following steps 3 - 5 of method two.

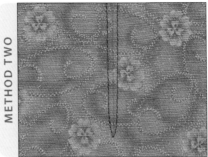

1. Unseamed opening. Staystitch along both sides of the line beginning and ending 3mm (1/8") from the raw edge and tapering to a point above the line.

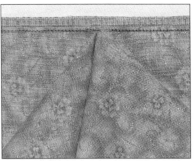

2. Cut the line to the point. Spread the cut edges. With right sides together, position the staystitching just above the stitchline on the placket. Pin and stitch.

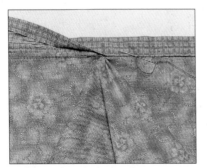

3. Press the placket and seam away. Press under the seam allowance on the remaining long raw edge. Fold the placket to the wrong side and pin. Handstitch to the previous stitchline.

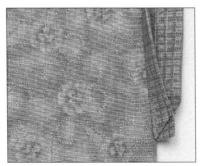

4. Press. On the wrong side, fold the placket in half, matching folded edges. Stitch diagonally across the end.

5. Depending on the overlap, left over right or vice versa, press one placket under and leave the other extending. Baste the underlap in position at the raw edge.

pleats

Pleats are measured folds created in the edge of the fabric. Unlike gathering, pleats are a structured, flat method of controlling fullness. They can be pressed into crisp creases or hang as soft folds. The folds in a pleat can be edgestitched to make them permanent, or just one section topstitched to hold the pleat in position.

For soft unpressed pleats, almost any fabric can be used successfully, but some fabrics hold crisp pleats better than others. Pleats hang more effectively and hold their shape longer if they are folded on the straight grain. Ensure you cut a piece of fabric strictly on the grain for multiple pleats, or try to fold an isolated pleat as close to the grain as possible.

The three main types of pleats are knife, box and inverted. Inverted and box pleats are the reverse side of the same fold formation. More complex pleating is best done by a professional.

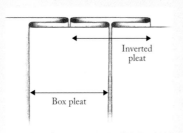

Inverted pleat

Box pleat

Pleats are formed by taking a foldline to meet a placement line. It is often better to use a pattern just to mark the positions of the lines on the top edge of the fabric. With the pattern removed, mark the lines with tacking following the threads in the fabric. Choose different coloured threads for the foldlines and placement lines to make them more distinct. Work on the right side to make it easier to match fabric patterns.

folded pleats knife pleats

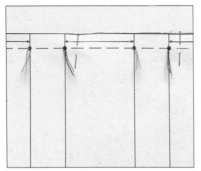

1. Using the pattern piece and a thread tack at the marks, mark the fold and placement positions on the upper edge.

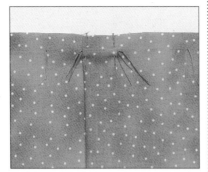

2. Take the fold mark to meet the placement mark for the first pleat and pin both sides of the pleat.

inverted pleat

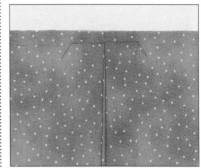

1. A pair of knife pleats folded towards each other creates an inverted pleat.

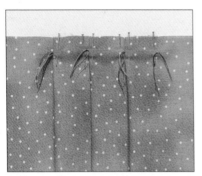

3. Repeat for any remaining pleats.

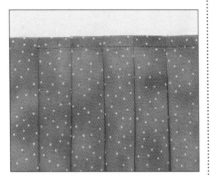

4. Baste in place just inside the stitchline. Press lightly from the wrong side along the upper edge.

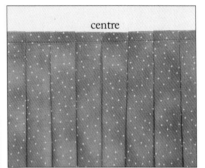

2. Knife pleats in opposite directions form an inverted pleat at the centre.

box pleat

pressed pleats

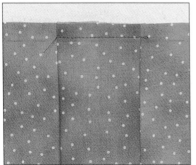

A box pleat is formed with two knife pleats folded away from each other.

Mark, fold and pin the pleats along the length following the grain. Tack in place. Press when the garment is complete.

hint pleating

If you have a number of pleats to form, make a cardboard or plastic pleating gauge to make measuring easier.

stitched pleats
knife pleats

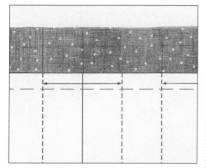

1. Following the grain of the fabric, mark the centre foldline and the left stitchline of each pleat on the wrong side of the fabric.

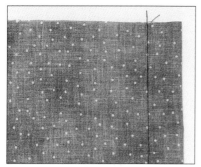

2. Fold the pleat with right sides together along the foldline. Stitch to the lower end of the stitched section of the pleat.

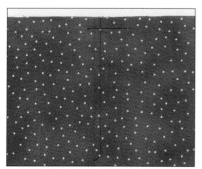

3. On the right side, position the pleat and press. Baste at the top edge. Top-stitch the pleat 6mm (1/4") from the seamed edge. At the lower end, stitch diagonally to the end of the pleat.

inverted pleats

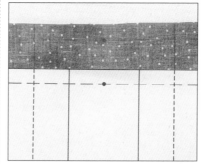

1. Mark the left and right stitchlines and the centre on the wrong side.

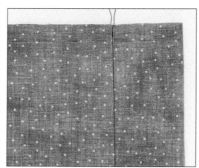

2. Matching stitchlines, fold the pleat right sides together on the centre mark. Stitch to the lower end of the stitched section of the pleat.

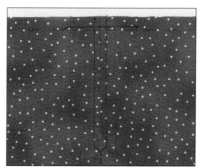

3. Pin the pleat matching the centre mark to the stitchline. Press. Topstitch along both sides, close to the fold and forming a point at the lower end.

box pleats

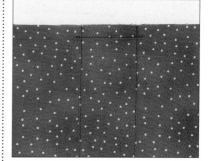

1. Form the pleat on the right side of the fabric in a similar manner to an inverted pleat. Top stitch along each side close to the fold.

hints pleating

The end of a stitched pleat is an area of great strain when the garment is worn. Stitch as securely as possible at this point.

To set the pleats, keep the tacking in place until after the garment is finished.

To prevent ridges on the right side, lay strips of thin card under the pleats when pressing after the garment is complete.

Check the fit before securing any pleats in position.

Fold and secure the hem before pressing pleats into their final position at the lower edge of a skirt.

pleats

pockets

Pockets first appeared as small concealed pouches to carry a handkerchief or a few coins. Over time pockets have evolved into a myriad of forms that are not only functional, but become part of the styling of a garment. Pockets can have a tailored or casual appearance, depending on their construction.

patch pockets

A patch pocket is simply a piece of fabric with finished edges, which is attached to the garment with machine stitching. They can be lined or unlined, plain or decorated, in basic or novelty shapes.

Preparation. Check the position of the pocket to ensure it is at a comfortable height. Adjust if necessary. Mark the pocket position, using tacked lines or a fabric marker appropriate for the fabric. Apply interfacing where required to add strength and stability.

unlined, squared lower edge

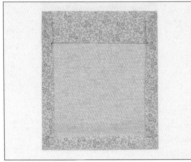

1. Turn under a double hem at the upper edge of the pocket and secure. Press under seam allowances along the sides, followed by the lower edge. Press diagonal folds on all corners of the seam allowances.

2. Tack the pocket in position on the garment. Beginning and ending with a triangle of stitching at the top corners, stitch along the outer edge of the pocket, leaving the upper edge open.

unlined, rounded lower edge

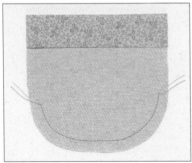

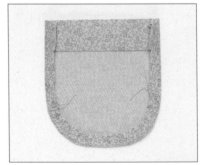

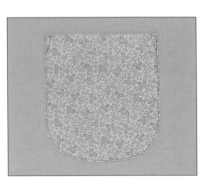

1. Fold and stitch the upper hem as before. Work a row of machine easing around the curved edges just outside the stitchline.

2. Pull on the ease stitching to roll the curved edge to the wrong side. The stitching should be just inside the fold. Press the seam allowance and diagonal folds under on the top corners.

3. Pin and tack the pocket in position. Stitch in place as before.

patch pocket with flap

A flap usually has the same styling as the pocket it is paired with. The following instructions show a flap with a rounded lower edge to match the pocket on the sample. Although other flaps may have a different shape, the method of attaching is the same. Flaps may also be attached without a pocket, as a design feature. They can also conceal the bound opening of an internal pocket.

Preparation

Form and attach the pocket following the previous instructions. Mark a line 1cm (³/₈") above the pocket.

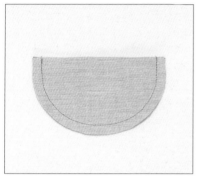

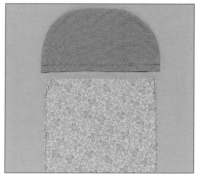

1. Apply interfacing to one flap piece. With right sides together and matching raw edges, pin the flap pieces together. Stitch around the sides and lower edge.

2. Trim the seam allowance and clip the curve. Turn to the right side and press. With the flap facing away from the pocket, pin and stitch in place, aligning the stitchline on the flap with the marked line.

3. Trim the seam allowance and clip the corners. Fold the flap down to cover the pocket. Stitch across the top of the flap, matching the stitching on the pocket.

---

hints patch pockets

To reinforce the stress points on the garment, fuse a piece of interfacing behind the upper corners before stitching the pocket in position.

Satin stitched bars are another method of reinforcing the ends of the stitching.

Triangular corner reinforcement

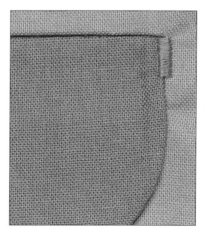

Satin stitch corner reinforcement

pockets

hip pocket

Front hip pockets are inserted into a seam at the sides and attached under a waistband along the upper edge. The upper edge of the pocket and the amount of fabric showing behind the opening, can be designed in many ways, but this style of pocket still consists of two main pieces, the pocket front and the pocket back.

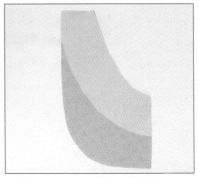

1. Apply a strip of non-fusible interfacing to the wrong side along the edge of the pocket front.

2. With right sides together, pin and stitch the pocket front to the garment piece along the edge.

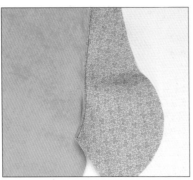

3. Trim the seam and clip the curve. Press the seam towards the pocket front and understitch along the edge.

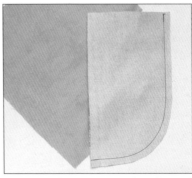

4. Fold with the seam on the edge and press. With right sides together, pin the pocket back to the outer edge of the pocket front. Stitch.

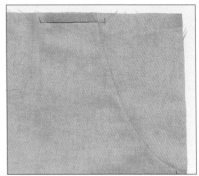

5. Trim the seam and neaten. Matching raw edges and marks, place all layers together at the top edge and baste in place.

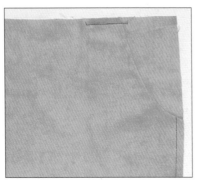

6. Repeat at the side. The front of the garment is now ready to have the back attached at the sides.

hints pockets

The pocket opening must be big enough for the hand to comfortably enter without placing too much strain on the attachment points.

If you have changed the position of a pocket, ensure the alterations are transferred to all pattern pieces involved.

in-seam pockets

These can be constructed in different ways.

In a separate in-seam pocket, additional pocket pieces are attached to the seam. The pockets can be cut from lighter weight fabric to reduce bulk inside the garment. In that case, cut a small facing of the garment fabric and attach it to the pocket opening to ensure the different fabric doesn't show, if the pocket gapes open.

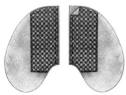

An integrated in-seam pocket is cut as part of the garment piece, so the seam is continuous inside the garment.

separate in-seam pocket

1. With right sides together and matching markings, pin a pocket piece to a garment piece. Stitch. Repeat for the remaining pocket and garment piece.

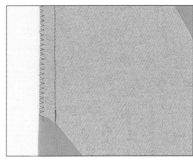

2. Neaten the raw edge for the depth of the pocket.

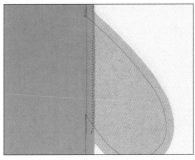

3. With right sides together, matching raw edges and markings, pin and stitch the garment and pocket pieces together, excluding the pocket opening.

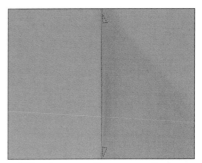

4. Trim the seam allowance and neaten. Press the pocket towards the front and reinforce the upper and lower ends of the opening.

integrated pocket

Preparation. Stitch staytape along the front opening edge of the pocket extension, just back from the stitchline.

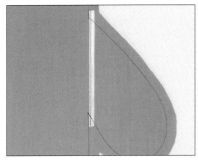

1. With right sides together and matching raw edges, pin the two sections of the garment together. Stitch the seam continuously, reinforcing the stitching at the top and lower points of the pocket.

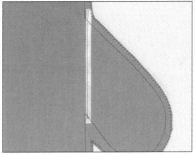

2. Trim the seam and neaten the raw edge.

3. Press the pocket towards the front and reinforce the upper and lower ends of the opening.

slashed pockets

Another form of pocket is constructed around a slash made in the garment. The cuts can be straight or slanted depending on the desired styling. The methods for neatening the cut edges and other design features, such as flaps and welts, are the only parts of the pockets visible on the right side. Inside, the pocket pieces are attached to the binding fabric.

pocket opening

Preparation. As with bound buttonholes, attention to detail in the marking and construction of these pockets is important to achieve a good finish of the garment piece. Mark the cutting line for the pocket on the right side.

Welted pockets

Bound pockets

Slashed pockets

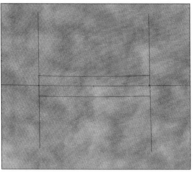

1. Mark lines at each end at right angles to the centre line. Extend all lines 4cm (1 1/2") past the cutting line. Mark another line 8mm (5/16") above and below the centre.

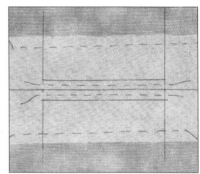

2. Repeat the markings on a piece of lightweight non-fusible interfacing and place behind the opening. Pin and tack around the outer edge and close to the centre line on both sides.

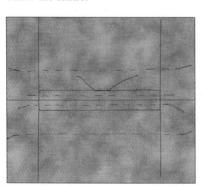

3. Beginning on one long edge and pivoting at the corners, staystitch around the opening.

hints slashed pockets

All stitching should be done with a short stitch length.

Press each step carefully. Leaving it to the final step will not set sharp edges.

Take the same number of stitches across the ends to ensure the distances are even.

pockets

bound pocket

A bound pocket adds a neat tailored finish to a pocket opening.

Preparation. Prepare the pocket opening on the garment piece. Cut two pocket pieces with rounded lower edges, each 2.5cm (1") wider than the finished width. Cut one piece the desired depth plus 7cm (2 3/4") - the second, the desired depth plus 3cm (1 1/4").

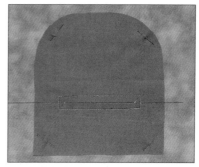

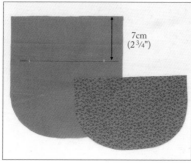

1. Rule a line across the wrong side of the larger piece at the desired depth. Rotate the pocket pieces before attaching to the garment.

2. Matching the pocket line with the centre line, pin the large pocket and garment right sides together. With the garment uppermost, stitch just outside the staystitching. Cut the centre line and diagonally into the corners.

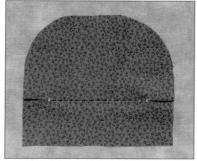

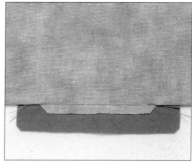

3. Push the pocket through to the wrong side. Roll the seam to the edge of the rectangle. Press. Fold the upper section down to form a pleat with the fold in the centre of the opening. Press.

4. Fold the lower section up to form another pleat in the same manner as before. Press. From the right side, secure the edges with tacking. Tack through the pleats near the stitching.

5. With the right side facing up, fold the garment piece back to expose one end of the pocket. Stitch across the end. Repeat on the remaining three edges of the opening. Press.

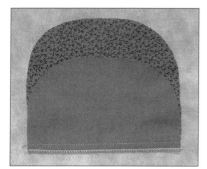

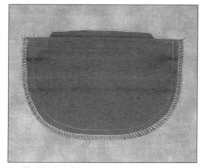

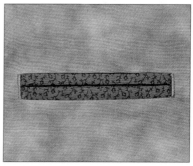

6. Stitch the remaining pocket piece to the straight edge of the large pocket. Trim the seam and neaten.

7. Fold the large pocket piece downwards. Trim the lower edges even if necessary. Pin the two layers together around the raw edges. Stitch and neaten.

8. On the right side, handstitch the ends to secure or stitch a bartack through all layers.

pockets

welted pockets A welt is a strip of fabric attached to the lower edge of the opening.

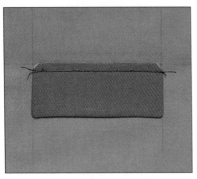

1. Cut two pocket pieces, each 2.5cm (1") wider than the finished width, adding 4cm (1½") to the desired depth. Rule a line across the wrong side of one piece at the desired depth.

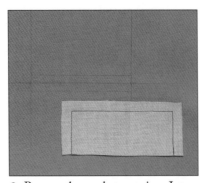

2. Prepare the pocket opening. Interface one welt piece. Pin the two welt pieces right sides together. Pivoting at the corners, stitch each end and one long edge.

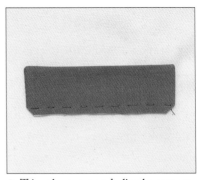

3. Trim the seam and clip the corners. Turn to the right side. Trim the seam allowance on the raw edges to 8mm (5/16") and clip the corner. Tack the raw edges together.

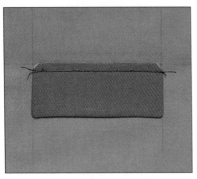

4. With the interfaced side of the welt facing the right side of the garment, pin and baste the welt to the lower edge of the marked opening.

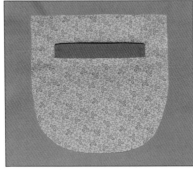

5. Sandwiching the welt, stitch the marked pocket piece to the opening, following steps 2 and 3 on page 117, omitting the pleat.

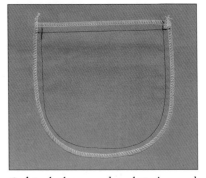

6. Attach the second pocket piece and finish the pocket following steps 6 and 7 on page 117. Press.

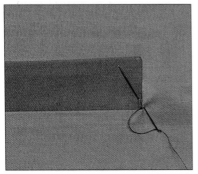

7. On the right side, position the welt to cover the opening. Handstitch the sides to the garment or edgestitch through all layers. Press.

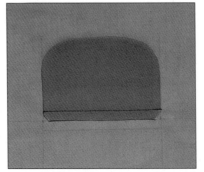

8. Pocket flap. Construct a flap and prepare a pocket opening as for the welted pocket. With the flap facing upwards, baste along the upper pocket stitchline.

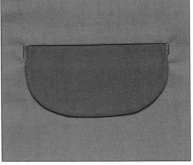

9. Finish the pocket following steps 6 and 7. On the right side handstitch or edgestitch the sides through all layers.

rouleau *also known as tubing*

Rouleau is a thin strip of fabric, which is seamed along the length and pulled to the right side using a tool such as a loop turner. It is often made from the same fabric as a garment and used in place of purchased cord. When the fabric used is cut on the bias, the tubing is very pliable and can be moulded to follow the contours of a shape or to form loops. If the rouleau is to be used as a tie, where it could be stretched or pulled tight, it is best made with fabric on the straight grain or the stitching might break.

Preparation. Cut a length of fabric on the bias, twice the finished width of the rouleau plus 12mm ($\frac{1}{2}$") for the seam allowances.

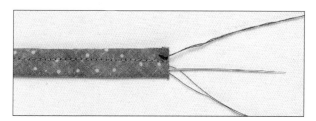

1. Matching raw edges, fold the strip right sides together along the length. Using a small straight stitch, stitch the entire length.

2. Trim the seam. Thread a large needle with a length of strong thread and double it. Ideally, the thread should be longer than the tube. Stitch the thread securely to the seam at one end.

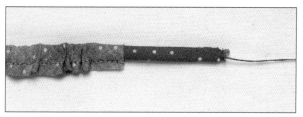

3. Drop the needle, eye end first, through the tube. Hold the tube vertically until the needle emerges at the opposite end. Pull gently, easing the tube through to the right side.

corded rouleau

Preparation. Cut a length of bias wide enough to wrap around the cord adding a 1cm ($\frac{3}{8}$") seam allowance on both long edges. Cut the cord at least twice as long as the fabric strip.

1. Beginning at the centre, wrap the fabric around the cord with right sides together and matching raw edges. Using a zipper foot and a small straight stitch, stitch as close as possible to the cord. Trim the seam to 3mm ($\frac{1}{8}$").

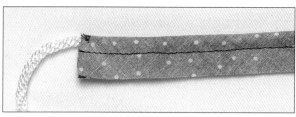

2. Handstitch the cord to the fabric at the centre point of the entire length of cord to secure.

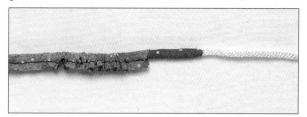

3. Easing the fabric backwards from the centre, pull the enclosed cord through the tubing to cover the free cord. Trim the excess cord.

ruffles

also known as frills

Ruffles are decorative strips of fabric, gathered or eased into a seam to produce fullness at the outer edge. There are two main types of ruffle. One is cut as a straight length of fabric and gathered to form a frill. The gathered ruffle can have one or both edges finished with plain narrow hems or a variety of decorative trims such as lace, braid or ribbon. To determine the length of fabric needed for a gathered ruffle, allow three times the finished length for full ruffles and twice the length for a softly gathered ruffle. It may be necessary to cut several strips of fabric and seam them together to achieve the right length. The second type is a circular piece of fabric cut with a short inner curve and a much longer outer curve. When the inner curve is straightened out and inserted into a seam, the outer curve falls into a soft ruffle.

single layer straight ruffles
plain ruffle

Preparation. Cut a strip of fabric the desired finished width, plus seam and hem allowances. Finish the hem.

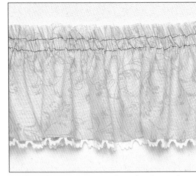 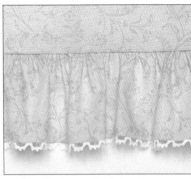

1. Stitch two rows of gathering along the upper edge of the ruffle. Pull on the bobbin threads to gather.

2. Attach the ruffle following steps 5 and 6 on page 85.

ruffle with a frilled heading

Preparation. Cut a strip of fabric the desired finished width, plus hem allowance on both sides. Neaten both raw edges using your desired method.

1. Stitch two rows of gathering between the upper and lower edges. The upper allowance is usually much smaller than the one below.

2. Pull on the bobbin threads to gather the ruffle. Stitch along the centre of the two gathering rows to secure the ruffle in position on the garment.

circular ruffle

Circular ruffles are particularly effective when made from softly draping fabrics. This type of ruffle is cut from a large circular shape with a smaller inner circle. The circumference of the inner circle is approximately the length of the edge where the ruffle is to be attached. The distance between the inner and outer edges is the finished depth of the ruffle plus hem and seam allowances. Cut the outer circle first and then along the straight grain through to the inner circle. Cut out the inner circle last.

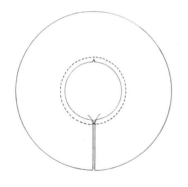

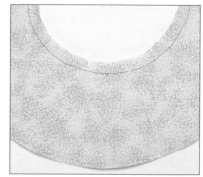

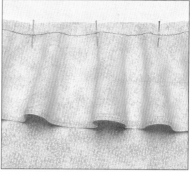

1. Staystitch the inner circle just inside the stitchline. Clip the inner seam allowance at close intervals to allow the edge to be straightened out. Neaten the outer raw edge using a rolled hem.

2. Mark the centre and quarters on the inner edge and the edge of the garment. With right sides together and matching raw edges, pin the ruffle to the garment edge at the marked points.

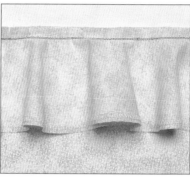

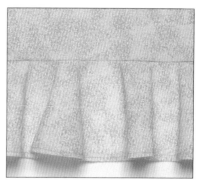

3. Pin between the sections, easing the ruffle to fit the edge. Baste in place. Stitch, ensuring no pleats form in the ruffle on the stitchline.

4. Trim the seam and neaten. Press the seam towards the garment.

hints **ruffles**

Ruffles can be an effective way to lengthen a garment.

Cut straight ruffles as a double layer when using sheer fabrics. this adds body and eliminates the need to neaten the lower edge.

ruffles

sashes

Sashes add a decorative element to the styling of a dress while controlling any excess fullness at the back. They can be constructed in various widths and from one or two layers of fabric. For a lighter finish, use a single layer which has been hemmed or finished on the sides and one end. The most common form of sash has a straight or diagonally finished end.

Sashes may also have shaped ends or be embellished with embroidery and lace. Embroidery and other forms of trimming are usually worked on a single layer of fabric before the sash is constructed.

Sashes are inserted into seams or darts on or near the sides of a dress. If the sash is wide, the end is gathered or pleated to reduce the width before attaching to the garment.

For each of the following methods make two sashes, ensuring they are a mirror image of each other.

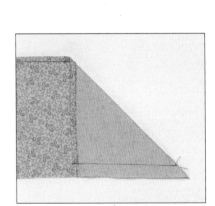

single layer sash

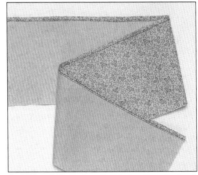

1. Cut a length of fabric the desired width plus seam allowances on all edges. Stitch a narrow double hem on one long raw edge.

2. At one end, fold the hemmed edge diagonally over to align the raw edges on the lower edge. Using the same seam allowance as the folded hem, stitch from the hem to the point.

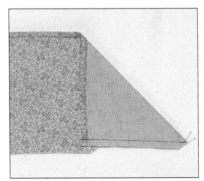

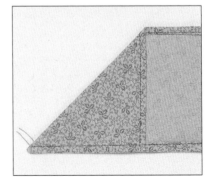

3. Trim the seam to within 1cm (³/₈") of the end of the stitching. Clip the point.

4. Turn the corner through to the right side. Forming a narrow double hem on the remaining raw edge, stitch from the point to the opposite end of the sash. Press.

folded double layer sash

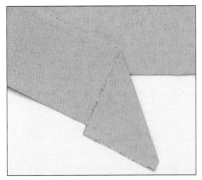

1. Cut the fabric, twice the desired width plus seam allowances. With right sides together, press the strip in half along the length. Fold one end diagonally, bringing the stitchline to meet the fold and press.

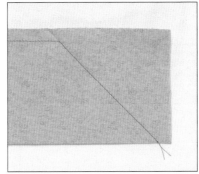

2. Unfold the diagonal end. Stitch the long raw edge and diagonally across the pressed fold at the end.

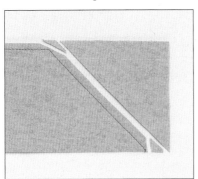

3. Trim the seams and clip the corners.

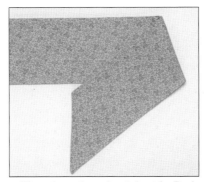

4. Turn through to the right side. Push out the corners carefully. Press.

attaching a sash

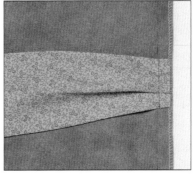

1. Fold pleats or gather the raw end of the sash to reduce the width. Baste the sash at the marked position on the garment.

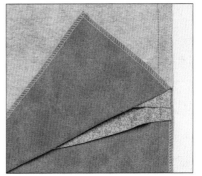

2. Attach the remaining section of the garment, sandwiching the sash in the seam.

hints attaching a sash

At times it may be necessary to attach a sash where there is no seam to conceal the end. In that case, stitch it to the fabric with the sash lying in the opposite direction.

Fold the sash in the correct direction and stitch to enclose the raw edge.

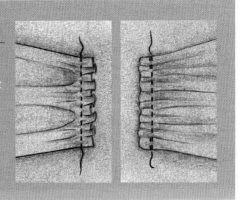

seams

A simple straight seam is the most common way to attach one piece of fabric to another. There are various other types to use when the garment styling demands a different seam. French and other self neatening seams are ideal for transparent fabrics. Flat fell seams provide strength as well as distinctive styling to casual clothing. Pattern instructions use a straight seam as the basis for all sewing, but will tell you when to use a different seam.

Careful preparation, accurate stitching and pressing, will produce a well-fitting garment with a neat finish. Place the pins horizontally, across the stitchline. This will enable you to stitch close to the pins and take them out easily as you reach them.

straight seam

In a well formed straight seam, all the stitching is exactly the same distance from the raw edge. A plain straight stitch, set to a length suited to the task is used. One exception is a straight seam on stretch fabric, where a special stretch stitch, set to a short length is better.

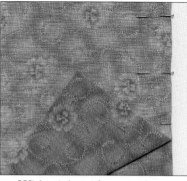

1. With right sides together and matching raw edges and markings, pin the two pieces of fabric together. Place the pins through the fabric on both sides of the stitchline and at right angles to the seam.

2. Tack close to the stitchline. As your confidence grows, tacking may not be necessary for some simple seams. Pinning will be sufficient. Stitch the seam, removing the pins as you go.

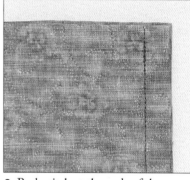

3. Back stitch at the ends of the seam, ensuring the stitching secures the section where an adjacent stitchline will cross the current seam.

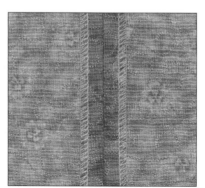

4. Remove the tacking. Neaten both sides of the seam separately and press open.

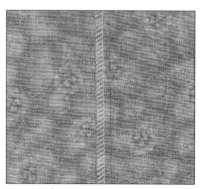

4a. Alternatively, trim the seam and neaten the raw edges together. Press to one side.

seam guide

The base plate of your machine has a series of numbered lines or seam guides. The distance between the needle in the centre position and each line, corresponds with the most common seam allowance widths. Feed the fabric through, aligning the edge with the appropriate seam guide to achieve an even seam. Keep your eye on the edge of the fabric, until you near the end of the seam.

Curves. Stitching around a curve requires careful guiding to keep the raw edges aligned with the seam guide. Stitching slowly is advisable to finish the seam in one smooth action. Avoid stopping to lift the presser foot and moving the fabric before proceeding, except on the tightest curves.

flat fell seam

This is a self neatening seam. A flat fell seam is particularly suited to side seams where extra strength is needed. When finished with topstitching, it can be decorative as well as functional. This seam requires a seam allowance of 1.5cm ($^5/_8$").

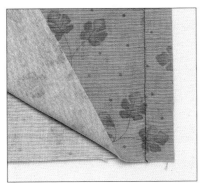

1. With wrong sides facing and matching markings, pin the two pieces together. Stitch the seam.

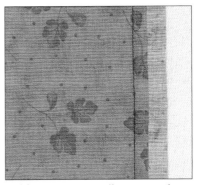

2. Trim one seam allowance only to 8mm ($^5/_{16}$").

3. Press the seam flat. Press the extending section of the wide seam allowance over the narrow, enclosing the raw edge.

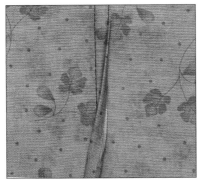

4. Open out the fabric. Rotate the fabric and press the seam to the right. Pin in place.

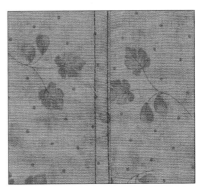

5. Work a line of edgestitching along the fold to secure the seam.

seams

self faced seam

This seam works best on lightweight fabrics that don't fray easily. It requires a seam allowance of 1.5cm (5/8").

1. With right sides facing and matching raw edges and markings, pin the fabric pieces together. Stitch the seam. Trim one seam allowance to 4mm (3/16").

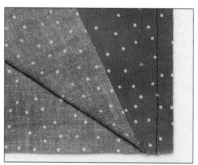

2. Press the seam flat. Press under 4mm (3/16") on the wide seam allowance.

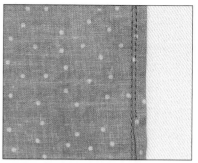

3. Bring the fold to meet the previous stitching, enclosing the raw edges. Edgestitch close to the fold. Press the seam to the right.

french seam

French seams create a beautiful finish on the inside of a garment. They are particularly suited to sheer fabrics, as the seam is sewn twice, fully enclosing the raw edges. To achieve a fine French seam, start with a seam allowance of 1cm (3/8").

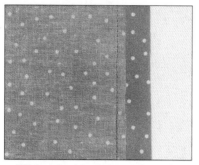

1. With wrong sides facing and matching markings, pin the fabric pieces together. Stitch the seam 5mm (3/16") from the raw edge.

2. Trim the seam allowance to 3mm (1/8"), ensuring that the edge is straight and even.

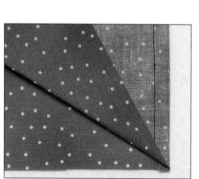

3. Press the seam flat and to one side. Fold the right sides together with the stitching on the fold. Press and pin. Stitch along the stitchline, enclosing the raw edges.

4. Press the seam flat and then to one side. Press again from the front.

hint stitching direction

Stitch with the grain where possible to minimise stretching and puckering.

Stitch opposing seams in the same direction on both sides of the garment, such as side seams from waist to hem and shoulder seams from neck to shoulder point.

finishing seams

To reduce bulk, seam allowances may require trimming or grading.

trimming

A seam allowance is often wider than its finished width to allow the seam to be stitched effectively. Pressed open, seams require little trimming. Other seams will require trimming to reduce bulk and to allow a smooth line on the outside. With the seam flat, trim through both fabric layers, ensuring the edge is straight.

grading

After trimming, the seam may need to be graded to further reduce bulk. Trim the layers of the seam allowance to different widths, leaving the longest to sit nearest the garment. This ensures the seam will not cause ridges when pressed.

clipping corners

Points may require several clips to allow them to sit flat when turned. The sharpness of the point will determine how many cuts are required.

1. An outward facing corner will only require one cut diagonally across the point.

2. An inward facing corner will require one cut diagonally into the point. Because this type of corner is stretched wide when turned through to the right side, it is advisable to stitch a row of staystitching just inside the seam allowance before cutting.

3. Trim a sharper point with at least three cuts, one diagonally across the corner as before and then two more to deepen the angle on both sides of the corner.

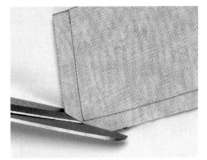

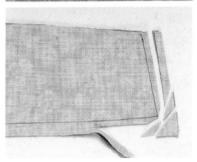

hint clipping

Clippng may weaken the corner on fragile fabrics. Omit the clipping and fold the corner instead. Before turning to the right side, fold and press the point followed by the sides.

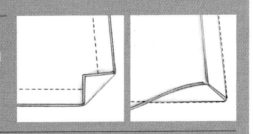

Clips into a corner should go closer to the stitchline than clipping to a seam, which is why it requires staystitching to stabilise the corner point.

seams

127

neatening seams

Aside from the self neatened seams, all seams with raw edges will require neatening to prevent the raw edges fraying and becoming unsightly and uncomfortable on the inside.

zigzag or overlock stitch

This is the easiest method to neaten a raw edge. It also has the advantage of keeping the edges of the seam flat, making it less likely to cause ridges on the right side when the seam is pressed.

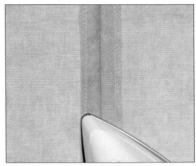

Open seams. Set the machine to a suitable stitch size. Trim the seam if necessary. Stitch along both edges of the seam separately. Press open.

Flat seams. Alternatively, trim the seam to 8mm ($^5/16$") and neaten with the raw edges together. Press to one side.

turned under

This form of neatening can be used when a zigzag stitch is not available. It should only be used for lightweight fabrics. Leave the seam allowance untrimmed. Press the seam open.

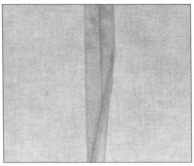

Fold under 3mm ($^1/8$") of the fabric on one raw edge and topstitch the fold on the right side. Repeat for the remaining raw edge. Press the seam again from the right side.

hint seams

The neatening method will depend partly on the fabric weight.

An open seam may show through on lightweight fabrics and should be kept narrow.

The seams on heavyweight fabrics are best neatened seperately and pressed flat.

bound seam

Binding a seam makes for a neat finish and is particularly suited to heavyweight fabrics. It requires a large seam allowance.

Preparation

Cut a strip of bias binding 4cm (1 $^1/2$") wide. Alternatively, use purchased bias binding. Stitch the seam and press open. Bind the raw edges of the seam following the instructions on page 39. Press the bound edges. On the right side, press the seam lightly.

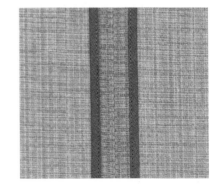

shirring

Shirring is a decorative band of gathering, worked in rows across the fabric. Shirring is both practical and a form of enhancement as it stretches to allow ease of dressing.

elastic shirring

Preparation. Wind the shirring elastic onto the bobbin by hand, stretching it slightly as you wind. Normal stitch length will allow the elastic to gather the fabric. Loosen the top tension slightly if possible. Mark the first line on the reverse side of the fabric, using an appropriate fabric marker. Finish the upper raw edge of the fabric if necessary.

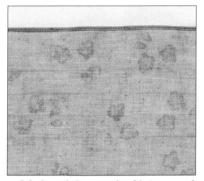

1. Mark each line on the fabric, spaced according to the pattern. Alternatively, use a quilting guide on the presser foot to space the successive rows of shirring.

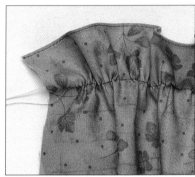

2. Leaving long tails at each end, stitch along the first line.

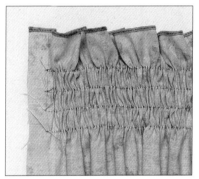

3. As you stitch each row stretch the elastic in previous rows to flatten the fabric. Pull on the elastic tails to adjust to fit the pattern. Pull the thread tails to the back in the seam allowance and tie with the elastic to secure.

gathered shirring

The rows of stitching would break with repeated wear and therefore require 'staying'. Subsequently, unlike elastic shirring, this method is set in its final position.

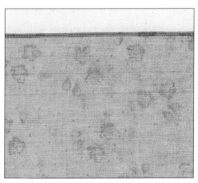

1. Prepare the fabric as before.

2. Work rows of gathering along each marked line. Pull up the gathers to fit. Stitch narrow braid behind each row.

sleeves

Set-in sleeves, are the most widely used sleeve type. They can have a smart, tailored look or appear slightly more casual depending on the method of construction or the whim of current day dress designers.

One other major style is the raglan sleeve. Raglan sleeves can have deep loose styling, making them suitable for coats and jackets designed to be worn over other clothing. T-shirts with close fitting raglan sleeves can hug the body quite firmly.

raglan sleeves

A raglan sleeve is attached to a garment with a seam running diagonally from the neckline, to the underarm. If using woven fabrics, there is usually a dart in the middle of the shoulder to take out the fullness at the top of the sleeve. The dart shapes the sleeve to match the shoulder line. This dart is not usually required on a raglan sleeve in knit fabric.

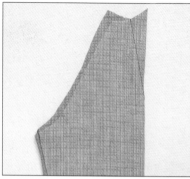

1. With right sides together and matching markings, pin and stitch the dart in the top of the sleeve if required.

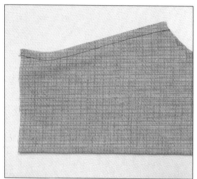

2. With right sides together and matching markings, stitch the sleeve underarm seam. Neaten the seam and press the seam open.

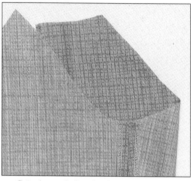

3. Stitch and finish the side seams in the bodice.

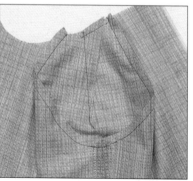

4. With right sides together and matching markings and seams, pin and stitch the sleeve into the armhole.

5. Trim and neaten the seam. Press towards the sleeve at the upper edges, leaving the underarm seams standing up.

set-in sleeve

A set-in sleeve with a smooth head, or cap, has a top curve which is slightly longer than the corresponding area of the armhole edge. Therefore the top edge of the sleeve has to be eased to fit the armhole. The aim of achieving a smooth sleeve head is not to form any pleats or gathers across the head. Sleeves with a softly gathered head have the fullness gathered into the armhole at the top, which is an easier technique to master.

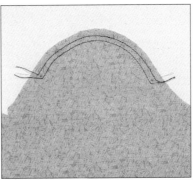

1. Stitch two easing rows across the head of the sleeve between the marks.

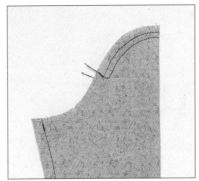

2. With right sides together, pin and stitch the underarm seam. Neaten and press the seam.

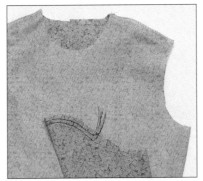

3. Turn the sleeve to the right side. Leave the prepared bodice right sides together.

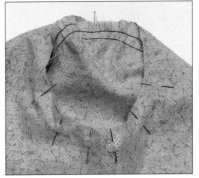

4. With right sides together and matching marks, pin the sleeve into the armhole along the lower curve between the ends of the easing. Place a pin matching the upper sleeve marking to the shoulder seam.

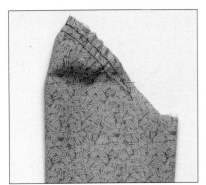

5. Pull up the easing until the sleeve fits the armhole. Ensure there are no gathers. Remove the sleeve and press it over a curved pressing surface.

6. Re-pin the sleeve to the armhole.

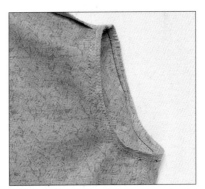

7. Tack in place. Stitch around the armhole overlapping at the under arm seam. Trim and neaten the seam.

8. Carefully press the seam towards the sleeve at the head using the tip of the iron.

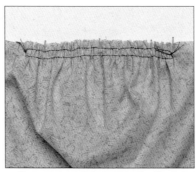

9. For a gathered sleeve head, adjust the gathering to fit the armhole in step 4 and secure. Finish following steps 7 and 8.

flat construction *also known as shirt sleeve method*

Sleeves with a less rounded cap, can be attached using the flat construction method.

This allows the sleeve to be sewn into the armhole before the underarm and side seams are stitched.

1. Stitch and finish the shoulder seams in the bodice.

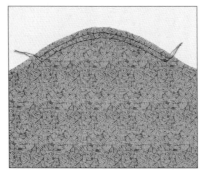

2. Stitch the rows of easing across the head of the sleeve.

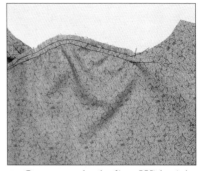

3. Open out the bodice. With right sides together and matching markings, pin the sleeve into the armhole. Ease to fit the armhole.

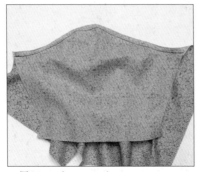

4. Trim and neaten the seam.

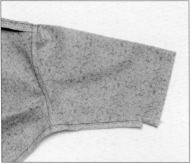

5. Matching sleeve seams, pin and stitch the underarm and side seams in a continuous line. Trim and neaten the seam.

6. Press towards the back. Finish the lower edge of the sleeve.

sleeves

sleeve finishes

A basic folded hem is the simplest method of neatening the lower edge of a sleeve. A facing, cut on the straight grain or the bias, is also a simple hemming method. This produces a firmer edge as the facing is turned under on a seam.

As well as being functional, more intricate sleeve finishes such as frills, bands, cuffs or bindings are usually a design feature of the garment. Often, their function is to control the fullness of the sleeve at the lower edge. A frill or a wide binding can also be used to lengthen a sleeve if it has been cut too short or after a child's growth spurt.

It is important to determine the correct length of a sleeve before constructing the finish at the lower edge. Refer to the instructions for lengthening and shortening patterns on page 18.

continuous sleeveband - *one piece*

Preparation

Apply interfacing to the wrong side of one half of the sleeveband. With wrong sides together, press the band in half. Unfold. Press under the seam allowance on the long raw edge of the uninterfaced half. Trim to 6mm (¼").

Work gathering rows on the sleeve if required.

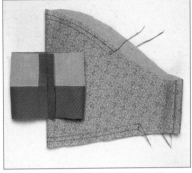

1. Stitch and finish the sleeve underarm seam. With right sides together, join the ends of the band to form a circle. Trim the seam and press open.

2. With right sides together and matching seams, pin and stitch the band to the lower edge of the sleeve. Trim the seam to 6mm (¼"). Press the band away from the sleeve.

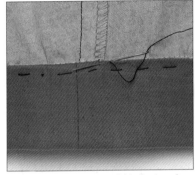

3. Matching seams, refold the band to the inside, aligning the folded edge with the previous stitchline. Pin, tack and handstitch in place.

4. Press carefully from the right side using the tip of the iron.

hint sleeve length

For a short puff sleeve, ensure the gathers begin and finish at the marked points on the sleeve head and lower edge. This will prevent the sleeve twisting out of shape.

sleeves

continuous sleeveband - *two piece*

1. Apply interfacing to one sleeveband piece. Press under the seam allowance on the long raw edge of the remaining sleeveband. Trim to 6mm ($1/4$").

2. With right sides together, join the ends of the sleevebands to form circles. Trim the seams and press open. Unfold the pressed edge.

3. With right sides together and matching seams, pin and stitch the band to the facing. Trim the seam and press the facing and seam away from the band. Attach the band following steps 2 - 4 of the one piece band.

piped sleevebands

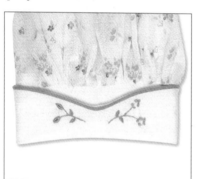

Piped and turned cuff with embroidery

Two piece band with piped edges

Two piece band with piping and lace frill

hints sleevebands

A folded hem on the lower edge of a sleeve is the only method that can be easily adjusted after it is complete. If a more complex sleeve finish has already been constructed at the lower edge and it becomes necessary to alter the length, take the sleeve out of the armhole and make the necessary adjustments to the sleeve head.

sleeves

elastic casing

Preparation

Stitch and finish the underarm seam in the sleeve. Cut a length of fabric on the bias to fit around the lower edge of the sleeve, adding 2cm (¾") at the ends. The width should be 6mm (¼") wider than the elastic plus 12mm (½") for seam allowances on the raw edges. Press 6mm (¼") to the wrong side on both long raw edges. Unfold.

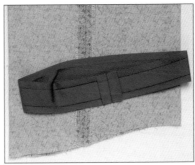

1. Using a 1cm (⅜") seam allowance and with right sides facing, stitch the ends of the casing together to form a circle. Press the seam open.

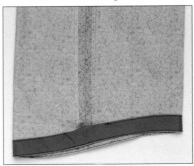

3. Rolling the seam to the edge, press the casing to the wrong side. Topstitch close to the edge. Leaving an opening at the seam, pin and stitch the upper edge of the casing close to the fold.

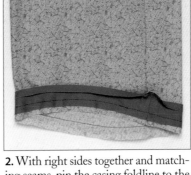

2. With right sides together and matching seams, pin the casing foldline to the sleeve stitchline. Stitch along the casing foldline. Trim the seam to 6mm (¼").

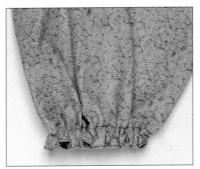

4. Insert the elastic and finish the casing following the instructions on page 55.

elastic casing with self-fabric frill

Cut and prepare the bias casing strip following the previous instructions, or use purchased bias binding.

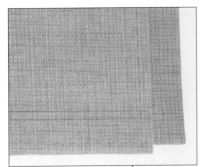

1. Mark a line across the lower edge of the sleeve, at the position for the casing. Mark another line half the finished width of the casing above the first line.

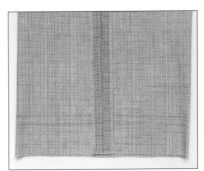

2. With right sides together, stitch the underarm seam of the sleeve. Neaten both sides of the seam separately and press open.

3. Neaten the lower edge of the sleeve. Attach the casing, insert the elastic and finish the casing following the instructions on page 57.

faced hem

Preparation. Stitch, neaten and press the underarm seam.

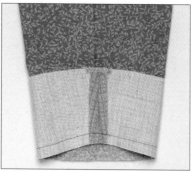

1. Cut a 5cm (2") wide facing, following the contour of the sleeve edge. With right sides together, stitch the facing seam. Press open and trim the seam allowances.

2. With right sides together and matching seams, pin and stitch the facing to the lower edge of the sleeve. Trim the seam to 6mm (¼").

3. Press the facing and seam away from the sleeve and understitch the seam. Press the facing to the wrong side. Handstitch the facing in place.

folded hem

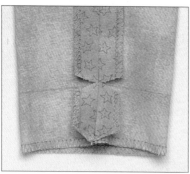

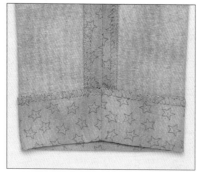

1. Mark the finished length of the sleeve with pins. Neaten the raw edge and press the hem to the wrong side. Unfold. Clip both sides of the seam at the fold.

2. Refold the hem and pin. Tack in place and handstitch to secure. Alternatively, machine stitch the hem with a single line of topstitching or twin needle stitching.

hints sleeves

Check sleeve and armhole for fit and adjust the pattern pieces if required.

Take care to transfer any pattern markings to the sleeve and the armhole edge of the garment pieces.

Use appropriate pressing techniques during construction.

lapped sleeveband

Also known as shirt style cuff

This tailored sleeveband is usually found on long sleeves to allow the sleeve to open at the wrist. The positioning of the button and buttonhole is important to close the band at the correct size.

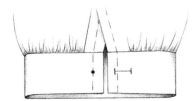

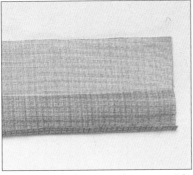

1. Apply interfacing to the wrong side of one half of the band. Press the band in half, wrong sides together. Unfold. Press under the seam allowance on the long raw edge of the uninterfaced half. Trim to 6mm (¼").

2. Construct a lapped placket at the marked position following the instructions page 108. Stitch, neaten and press the underarm seam. Prepare the lower edge of the sleeve following the pattern instructions.

3. With right sides together and matching markings, pin the upper edge of the band to the sleeve with the seam allowance extending past the opening. Adjust the sleeve to fit. Stitch, securing the ends.

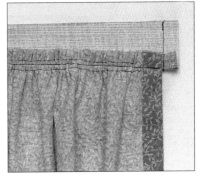

4. Trim the seam to 6mm (¼"). Press towards the band. Fold the band right sides together, matching the folded edge to the seam. Stitch across the end level with the placket edge.

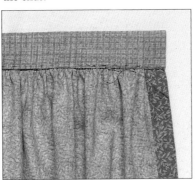

5. Turn the band to the right side aligning the folded edge with the previous stitchline. Tack in place and handstitch.

6. Press carefully from the right side.

topstitching

Topstitching is a collective term used for rows of machine stitching worked on the right side to define a seam or folded edge. While the stitching is usually ornamental, it also has a practical function, securing and strengthening a seamline, or preventing a facing or lining from rolling to the right side and become visible.

Pleats can be topstitched to make the folds permanent or to

strengthen the seamed section. Flat fell seams are topstitched to secure and reinforce them.

Topstitching is worked at an even distance from the fold or seam, using a longer than normal stitch length and sometimes stronger thread. The thread colour can be matching or contrasting, depending on the desired effect. It can be a single or double line of stitching. Triple lines of topstitching are sometimes a feature on the side seams of jeans.

If the topstitching distance is the same as any of the seam guides on the machine, use these to position the stitching. The following instructions use the distance between the needle and the edge of the presser foot to place a row of topstitching 6mm (¼") from the edge. To adjust the width, adjust the position of the needle.

To prevent the layers of fabric from moving, it may be helpful to place a line of tacking a short distance from where the topstitching will be placed.

1. Position the garment edge under the needle at the desired position. Lower the presser foot.

2. Stitch an even distance from the edge. As you near a corner, place a pin in the fabric the same distance from the following edge. Stitch to within one stitch of the pin.

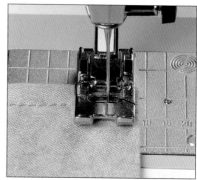

3. Remove the pin. Turn the fly wheel by hand to work the last stitch. Lift the presser foot and pivot with the needle in the fabric, re-aligning the next edge. Continue stitching.

hint topstitching

If you require a particular distance that can not be judged by any other method, measure from the needle to a point on the stitch plate. Rule a line with a lead pencil or place a piece of tape on the stitch plate to use as a guide.

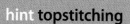
topstitching

edgestitching

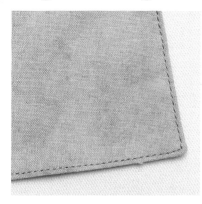

As the name suggests, this is a row of stitching placed close to an edge. Prepare and press the seam. Tack if necessary a short distance away from the position of the stitching. Stitch through all layers, close to the edge.

hint edgestitching

It may be difficult to keep the stitching straight as the presser foot is suspended above the stitch plate on one side. A special edge stitching foot, which is higher on one side, can help to alleviate the problem.

understitching

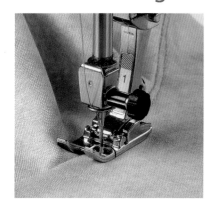

Understitching is a line of stitching worked close to a seam to prevent a facing or lining from rolling to the front. Once the seam is stitched, trimmed, graded and clipped, it is pressed towards the fabric layer where the understitching is to be placed. Stitch through all layers, 3mm (1/8") from the seam. If you are understitching a curve, keep the fabric flat in front of the presser foot and feed through without puckering.

decorative topstitching

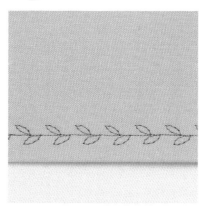

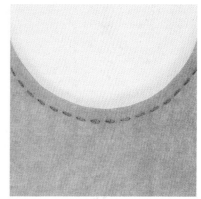

Combined edgestitching and topstitching

Decorative machine embroidery stitches

Running stitch worked by hand

topstitching

tucks

A tuck is a stitched fold in fabric, used to control fullness. Tucks also have practical purposes when formed as part of the styling to allow for growth. The width of a tuck is the measurement between the fold and the stitching. This can vary, along with the spacing between the tucks, according to the styling of a garment. Tucks hold their shape without twisting or puckering when formed and stitched on the straight grain.

Tucks are named according to the method of stitching or the spacing between them. The fold of a blind tuck meets or just covers the stitchline of the tuck beside it. Pintucks are so named because the width between the fold and the stitchline should be the width of a pin. Twin-needle pintucks are a simplified method of stitching these tiny tucks using a special machine needle with two needle shafts on a single shank.

marking tucks

Tuck positions are usually marked on a pattern piece, or a tucking guide is given if the tucks are stitched on a panel of fabric before the final shape is cut out. Use the pattern piece or tucking guide to mark the upper and lower positions of the tuck foldlines and then remove. Rule a line between the marks beginning at the top edge and following a thread in the fabric to the lower mark, using an appropriate fabric marker.

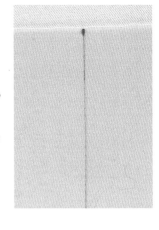

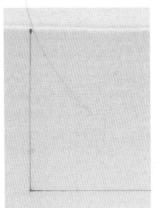

A vertical line, marking the first tuck foldline and a horizontal line marking the depth of the tucks, will be sufficient if you are using a spacing guide. Alternatively all the stitchlines can be marked or the tuck width gauged as you stitch by using one of the following methods.

stitching tucks

Gauging the width

1. Align the foldline with one of the seam allowance marks on the base plate, if they match the desired width of the tuck.

2. Place a piece of tape on the base plate beside the presser foot at the width of the tuck.

Gauging spacing between tucks

1. Use a spacing guide on the presser foot, with the bar adjusted to the width between the tucks.

2. For twin-needle pintucks, use the ridges beneath the presser foot as a guide for spacing.

basic tucks

For tucks covering the full distance of a pattern piece, the stitching can be secured inside the seam allowance at both ends. Leave the thread tails unsecured if the tuck finishes before the edge. With wrong sides together, fold the fabric on the foldline and press the fold. Stitch the tuck. Press the tuck flat and then to one side. Stitch all the tucks in the same manner, working each tuck in the opposite direction to the previous, to prevent the fabric from distorting.

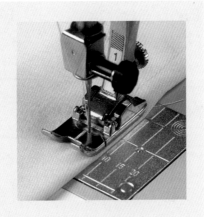

crossed tucks

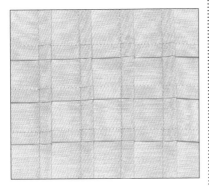

Mark and stitch all vertical tucks and press in one direction. Rotate the fabric keeping the first set of tucks facing downwards. Stitch the crossing tucks.

It is important to alternate the direction of the stitching for each tuck to prevent the panel becoming distorted. Press the crosswise tucks carefully to one side with the tip of the iron.

pintucks

1. Fold the fabric on the marked line. Edgestitch close to the fold.

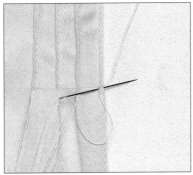

2. Fold and stitch remaining tucks. Take the top and bobbin threads separately to the wrong side at the end of the stitching.

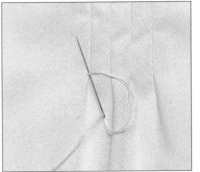

3. Wrong side. Place both in the needle and take several tiny back stitches through the fabric, ensuring the stitching doesn't show on the right side.

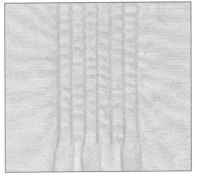

4. Press the tucks in the same direction.

tucks

twin needle pintucks

These delicate pintucks work best on lightweight fabrics.

Preparation. Mark the positions for the stitching following the previous instructions. In the following steps, the tucks are spaced using the ridges under the presser foot as a guide.

1. Holding the threads at the beginning to engage the bobbin, stitch along the first marked line.

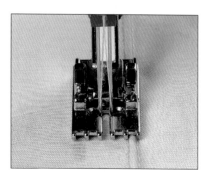

2. Stitch the next tuck, aligning the first tuck in a groove in the presser foot. Alternatively, follow a marked line.

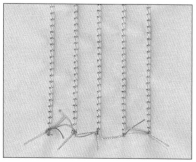

3. **Wrong side.** To secure the thread tails, take to back separately at the end of the tuck. Tie the top and bobbin threads together snugly against the fabric. Trim leaving short tails.

crossed

1. Mark the centre tuck in both directions. Stitch the first vertical tuck on the marked line. Using a spacer bar stitch all vertical tucks, working from the first.

2. Beginning with the centre line, stitch the horizontal tucks in the same manner to complete the grid.

turning a corner

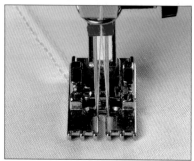

1. Stitch to the corner and stop with the needles in the fabric. Lift the presser foot. Leaving the needles in the fabric, carefully rotate the fabric 45°. Lower the presser foot again.

2. Work one stitch, turning the fly-wheel by hand. Stop with the needles in the fabric. Rotate as before, aligning foot in next direction. Lower the presser foot again.

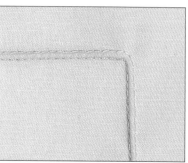

3. Continue sewing in the new direction.

corded pintucks

Use preshrunk no. 8 perle cotton in a colour to match the fabric or a darker shade for a shadow effect. A cording presser foot is used on the machine. This type of tuck is only suitable for areas where both ends can be secured in a seam to hold the cord in place.

Preparation. Secure the end of the cord on the wrong side at the start of the line. Position the fabric under the presser foot, holding the cord straight. Lower the needles with the cord centred between them. Stitch along the cord.

waistbands

Most waistbands are firm, structured finishes intended to secure the waistline of a garment at the correct position on the body.

There are two main types of waistband for skirts and trousers – straight or contoured. Straight waistbands are usually the same length as the circumference of the waist, plus a little extra for ease of wearing. Generally they are no wider than 5cm (2") when finished. Contoured waistbands

follow the curves of the body between the waistline and the rib-cage or the waistline and the hips.

For each of the following methods, construct the garment, including the zip closure, pockets, darts and lining if required. The upper edge of the garment will be slightly bigger than the matching distance between the markings on the waistband and will require easing to fit. Work a row of staystitching along the upper edge of the garment.

tucks

straight waistband

Preparation. Cut out the waistband and interfacing. A straight waistband should be marked at centre front, centre back and side seams. Transfer the markings to the interfacing and apply it to the wrong side of the waistband.

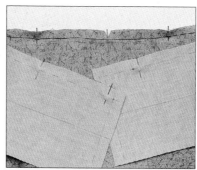

1. With the seam allowance extending at the front edge and matching marks, pin the waistband to the upper edge of the garment at the ends, centres and seams.

2. Continue pinning between the marks, easing the uper edge of the garment to fit the waistband. Tack and stitch in place.

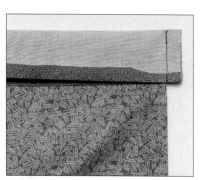

3. Trim the seam to 6mm (¼"). Press under the seam allowance on the remaining long edge and trim to 6mm (¼"). Fold the band right sides together at the overlap end. Stitch across the end.

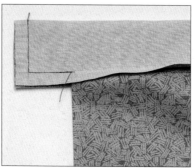

4. At the underlap end, place the band right sides together with the seam allowances unfolded. Beginning at the opening and pivoting at the corner, stitch around the end of the waistband.

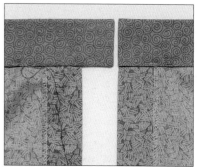

5. Trim the seams and clip the corners. Turn the ends to the right side, pushing out the corners. Matching markings, pin the folded edge of the waistband to the stitchline. Handstitch to secure. Press.

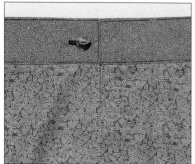

6. Work the buttonhole and attach the button to correspond. Alternatively, attach a hook and bar for a concealed closure.

contoured waistband

The method of attaching this is similar to a straight waistband.

Preparation. Apply interfacing to the wrong side of the facing pieces. Transfer markings to the interfacing. Stitch the front and back pieces together at the side seams and press open.

With right sides together, and matching centres and seams, pin and stitch the facing to the waistband at the upper edge. Attach the waistband following the previous steps.

faced waistline

An alternative to a waistband is a faced waistline. A facing is the easiest method to finish an edge that requires shaping. The facings are usually flat, as they have been drafted to fit the finished hip and waistline curves.

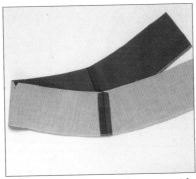

1. Apply interfacing to the wrong side of the facing pieces. With right sides together, stitch the side seams. Trim and press open. Neaten the lower edge.

2. With the seam allowance extending at both ends and matching markings, pin the facing to the upper edge of the garment at the ends, centres and seams.

3. Continue pinning between the marks, easing the upper edge of the garment to fit the waistband. Tack and stitch in place.

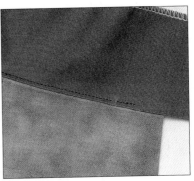

4. Trim the seam and clip the curve. Press the facing and seam away from the garment. Understitch close to the seam on the facing.

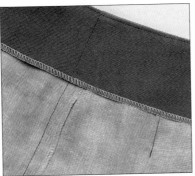

5. Fold under the extending ends of the facing at a slight angle. Fold the facing to the wrong side.

6. Handstitch the facing to the side seams and darts and along the opening edge.

waistbands

zips

Zips are an efficient and secure way to close an opening. They can be almost invisible when inserted into a seam, or attached using an exposed method to create a casual look.

Zips may be centred under the opening, offset to one side or set into the seam from the wrong side using a special presser foot.

Choose a zip suitable for the style of the opening and the weight of the fabric. If you are unable to find a zip to match the colour of the garment, choose one a shade darker to ensure it will remain inconspicuous.

attaching a centred zip

The position of the top end of the zip for this method depends on the final finish of the opening. If a facing is to be used, such as a neckline, you should place the upper stop 1cm (³/₈") below the stitchline of the garment. If the end is to be placed under a band, such as a skirt waistband, the upper stop should be close to the stitchline.

Place the zip presser foot on the machine.

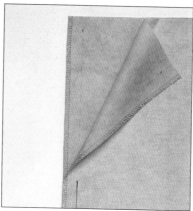

1. Securing the ends, stitch the garment seam to the marked point for the end of the zip. Neaten both sides of the seam separately.

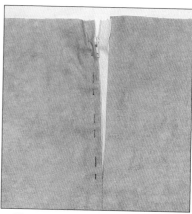

2. Press the seam open, including the opening for the zip. Pin the zip in position, centred on the opening. Splay the top ends of the zip open slightly, keeping the fabric folds aligned.

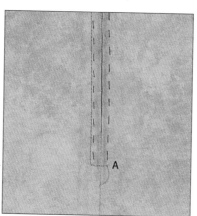

3. Tack close to the stitchline. Starting at A and pivoting at the corner, stitch across the lower end and along one side 6mm (¹/₄") from the opening.

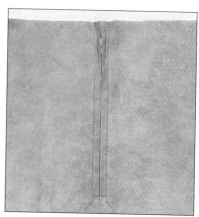

4. Return to the lower end and stitch the remaining side in the same manner. Press from the wrong side on a well padded board.

lapped zip

Use this method to attach a zip when it is placed at the side of a garment. To conceal the opening from the front, the lapped section is placed on the leading, or front edge. The placement of the top end of the zip is the same as the centered method. The instructions show a zip set into the left side seam.

Preparation. Stitch, neaten and press the seam open following step 1 of the centred zip.

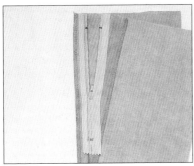

1. With right sides together and the zip closed, pin the right hand side of the zip to the corresponding side of the opening. Stitch in place.

2. Turn to the right side. Pin the fold close to the teeth. Pin the remaining side of the zip in place, with the lap slightly covering the fold on the right hand side.

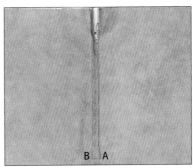

3. Tack in place. Starting at A topstitch across the base, pivot and stitch along the opening 1cm (³⁄₈") from the fold. Starting at B edgestitch the remaining side to the top.

open-end zip

This type of zip is used mostly in the front opening of casual jackets.

Preparation. Finish the lower edge of the opening. Finish the upper edge if required. Neaten the raw edges of the opening. Mark the stitchlines with a fabric marker or by pressing a foldline. Place the zip presser foot on the machine. Separate the zip.

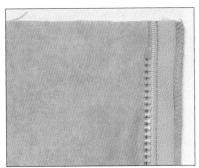

1. With right sides together, pin and stitch the left hand side of the zip onto the corresponding opening, aligning the stitchline close to the teeth.

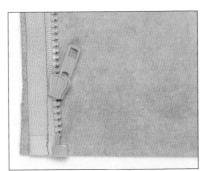

2. On the right hand side, stitch from the lower end with the slider at the top. Halfway along, stop with the needle just in the fabric. Lift the presser foot. Take the slider past the needle. Lower the foot and complete the stitching.

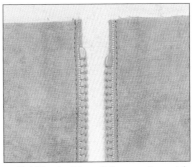

3. Fold both sides of the opening with the teeth on the edge. Stitch close to the fold on the right side. Work another row of stitching 4mm (³⁄₁₆") away from the first row if required for added strength.

zips

fly front

The following technique is used to insert a zip in the centre front of a pair of trousers. An extension, or shield is formed behind the zip to prevent undergarments getting caught in the teeth, as the slider is moved up or down. The method of overlap has traditionally followed the same rules as a button closure - right over left for women and left over right for men - but the accepted generic position for both is now left over right.

Preparation

Apply interfacing to the fly facing and one fly shield piece.

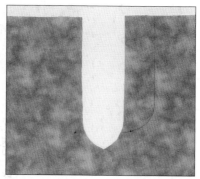

1. Mark the ends of the crotch seam and the topstitching line on the right hand piece.

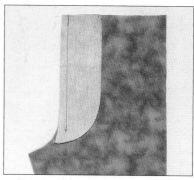

2. Neaten the straight edge of the fly facing. Pin and stitch the facing to the right hand side of the opening.

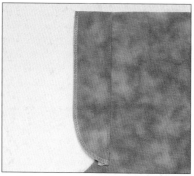

3. Trim the seam and turn to the right side. Fold the facing and seam away from the garment. Understitch to the top of the crotch seam.

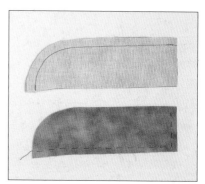

4. With right sides together, stitch the curved edge of the shield pieces. Trim the seam, notch the curve. Turn to the right side and press. Tack the raw edges together.

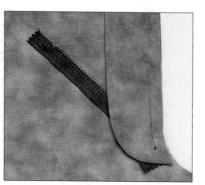

5. Aligning stitchlines, baste the zip to the right hand opening. Matching raw edges, pin and stitch the fly shield over the zip. Trim the seam and neaten.

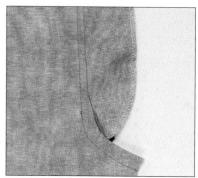

6. With right sides together, matching marks and keeping the facing and shield out of the way, stitch the crotch seam securely.

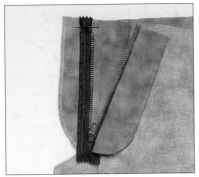

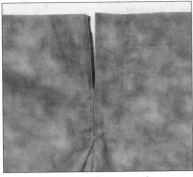

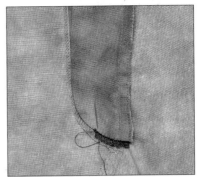

7. Pin and tack the remaining side of the zip to the facing, placing the teeth 4mm (³/₁₆") from the seam. Stitch along the centre of the tape.

8. Reposition the facing on the wrong side. Keeping the fly shield out of the way, topstitch from the upper edge to the crotch seam.

9. On the wrong side, handstitch the fly shield to the lower end of the zip.

securing the upper end

When setting a zip into an opening with both ends closed, such as a cushion back or the side seam in a dress, the tapes at the upper end of the zip should be stitched closed to take the strain off the stitching in the seam.

shortening a zip

If you have a zip just the right colour and style, but too long for the opening, it is possible to shorten it using the following method. Measure the required length. Whip over the closed zip at the marked position by hand or machine. Cut off the excess, 2cm (¾") below the stitching if required.

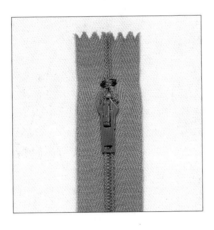

hint zips

When stitching the seam, use a zipper foot to get as close as possible to the zip stitching.

For the fly front and invisible zip methods, where the seam below the zip opening is stitched after the zip is inserted, use a standard zipper foot to stitch that seam. This will enable you to place the stitching close against the end of the zip.

zips

invisible zip

also known as concealed zip

This type of zip is attached using a particular presser foot.

As each foot may differ slightly for different machine brands, follow the manufacturer's instructions.

The positioning of the upper end of the zip is the same as the centred zip. Stitch the seam below the seam after the zip is inserted.

Always use a zip approximately 3cm (1 ¼") longer than the required opening.

This is because you only can stitch to a certain point, before the zipper foot is stopped by the zip slider, causing a small amount of zip to be unstitched.

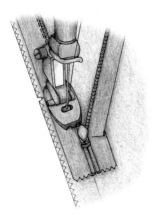

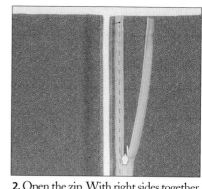

1. Neaten both sides of the seam allowance separately. Mark the lower end of the zip and the stitchlines on both sides of the opening.

2. Open the zip. With right sides together and aligning the coil with the stitchline, pin and tack the right hand edge on the right hand side of the opening.

3. Fit the coil into the right hand groove of the presser foot. Stitch from the upper edge to the lowest position possible.

4. Matching the marked ends of the seam, pin, tack and stitch the left hand side of the zip to the remaining edge of the opening. The coil sits in the left hand groove of the foot.

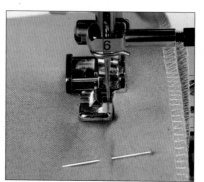

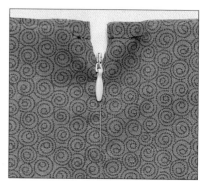

5. Close the zip. Pin the garment pieces with right sides together. Using a standard zipper foot, stitch the seam, beginning at the lower end of the zip. Press open.

6. Shorten the zip if required. Baste the edges of the tape to the seam allowance only.

glossary of terms

Appliqué Cut out shapes attached to a base layer of fabric, forming a design or pattern

Alteration Changes made to a pattern or garment to customise the fit

Awl Pointed tipped tool with a graduated shaft - used to pierce holes in fabric

Backing The last layer of fabric behind others

Back stitch Handstitch, used decoratively or to stitch seams

Reverse machine stitching used at the beginning and end of a seam to secure the stitching

Ballpoint needle Machine needle with a slightly rounded tip - used when stitching knit fabric

Basting *or tacking*
Long machine straight stitch worked to temporarily join or attach - removed when permanent stitching is in place

Binding Strips of fabric used to encase raw edges

Blind hem Machine hemming technique using a special presser foot, a blind hem stitch

Bobbin The spool holding the lower thread in a sewing machine

Bodice The section of a garment worn on the upper part of the body, from shoulder to waist

Bodkin Tool used to thread elastic through a casing

Boning Narrow nylon or plastic strips used to create structure and shape in fitted garments

Braid Flat decorative trim, usually containing some surface texture

Buckle Fastening used to secure a belt or tie

Bust line Horizontal line running around the fullest part of the bust and across the back

Bust point Point on the pattern where the tip of the bust should sit when wearing a garment

Buttonhole Neatened opening for a button to pass through

Buttonhole stitch Handstitch used to neaten the raw edges of a buttonhole. It resembles blanket stitch but has a looped edge

Cap sleeve Narrow short sleeve forming a cap over the top of the shoulder

Casing Channel of fabric used to enfold elastic or a drawstring

Clipping Cuts made into the seam allowance of an inward facing curved seam

Couching Securing cord, heavy threads or other narrow trims to a background fabric with stitching

Covered button Special button manufactured to be covered with fabric

Contoured Pattern pieces cut to fit the curve of the body, enabling them to sit flat when worn

Cutting line Outermost line of a pattern piece - the line to follow when cutting out the pieces

Dart Tapered fold stitched to help shape a garment to follow the contours of the body

Dress form *or dressmaker's dummy*
A dummy torso with adjustable sections, used to fit a garment to particular measurements during construction

Double hem Folding the fabric over twice to form a hem - the first fold to neaten the raw edge and the second, to the depth of the finished hem

Ease Small amount of excess fabric built into certain areas to allow for movement or to permit one edge to be shaped to fit another

Ease stitching Row of machine stitching just within the seam allowance used to adjust the ease in the seam

Edgestitch A row of topstitching very close to the edge of a fold or seam

Eyelet Small neatened hole in the fabric, often found in embroidery designs

Tiny metal rings punched through the fabric

Extension Piece extending past an edge of a garment or a separate piece added to enlarge or lengthen an area

Facing Piece of fabric used to finish a raw edge

Feed The mechanical movement of fabric over the stitch plate

Feed dogs Metal teeth protruding through slots in the stitch plate - they move up and down to push the fabric under the presser foot

Finger press Squeezing a fold or seam between the thumb and forefinger, while rolling it or pulling it through the fingers

Finished edge Any edge, visible or invisible, that has been seamed or neatened

Finished width The actual width of any garment section after the seams are stitched, turned and all allowances used

Foldline Line on a pattern piece indicating a point where the garment piece will be folded

Free motion Lowering the feed dogs to disengage the automatic feed, enabling the fabric to move in any direction

French seam Self finishing seam – one seam enclosing another

Frills *(see ruffle)*

Fusible Material with a film of adhesive on one side that can be bonded to fabric using heat

French curve A drafting ruler used to create curves when adapting patterns

Gathering Method of controlling fullness when a length of fabric is attached to a shorter edge

Grain *Lengthwise* grain (the warp) are the threads that run lengthwise, parallel to the selvedge

Crosswise grain (the weft) are the threads that run horizontally from selvedge to selvedge

Bias applies to any diagonal direction on the fabric. True bias runs at a 45° angle to the lengthwise and crosswise grain

Grading Trimming back the individual layers of the seam allowance to different widths, reducing the bulk in the seam

Gusset Square or diamond shaped piece of fabric sewn into intersecting seamlines to provide room for movement

Heading *or flange* Seam allowance on trim – should not be visible after the seam is complete

Hem Fabric turned up on the edge of the garment to provide a neat finished edge

Hip The fullest part of the hipline around the body

Hong Kong seam Flat seam with binding used to encase and neaten the raw edge

Hook and eye Closure that consists of the hook and a loop

Inside leg seam Seam between the legs, running from the crotch to the hem

Interfacing Layer of fabric or stabiliser applied to the wrong side of fabric to provide stability

Interlining *or underlining* Layer of lining fabric tacked to the wrong side of the garment pieces and integrated into the seams during construction

Inverted pleat Pair of mirror image knife pleats folded towards each other

Kick pleat An inverted pleat folded into an opening at the lower end of the centre back seam of a straight skirt

Kimono sleeve *also dolman, Magyar or integrated sleeve* Sleeve cut as an extension of the front and back bodice pieces

Knife pleat Folded tuck in the fabric, pressed to one side

Lining Layer of fabric used to cover or protect the inner surface of a garment - usually a separate inner layer made as a mirror image of the outer layer

Mandarin collar *also Chinese or Nehru collar* Short standing collar extending vertically from the neckline - often with rounded corners at the front

Marking Temporary marks made on the right or wrong side of the fabric - used to transfer the position of pattern markings

Mitre Method of neatly folding hems or flat trims so that they form a precise diagonal corner

Nape The upper back part of the neck below the hairline

Needle threader Looped wire used to pull thread through the eye of a needle

Notches Triangular or diamond shapes appearing on the cutting lines of a pattern piece - used to match positions when garment pieces are placed together

Notching Triangular shapes cut into outward facing curved seams

Notions Group of trimming and haberdashery items used in the construction of garments

Open end zip Zipper that separates into two parts allowing part of the garment to open completely

Overcasting or *whipping*
Strong handstitch used for holding a fold in position or joining two edges together

Overlocker or *serger*
Machine used for neatening the raw edge of a seam - trimming and overcasting the edge and sewing, all in one action

Overlock stitch Machine overcast stitch that encloses a raw edge to prevent fraying

Pattern Templates needed to cut out the individual sections of a garment. Dress patterns usually contain pattern pieces printed on tissue or plain white paper and include instructions to cut out and construct a particular garment

Peter Pan collar Usually a one piece collar with rounded ends at the centre front - can also appear as two pieces with round ends at the front and back

Petersham Heavy weight woven band with a line of reinforced stitching to prevent it from folding or rolling when stitched into a waistband

Pile or *nap*
Describes the surface texture of short cut fibres incorporated into the weave of the fabric, producing a soft plush surface

Pilling Tiny balls of fibre occurring on the surface of some fabrics after repeated wear and laundering

Pintucks Narrow tucks stitched in rows on the fabric to add decorative detail

Piping Made from a thin cord encased in a strip of fabric

Pivot Rotating fabric with raised presser foot and needle in fabric

Placket Additional piece added to partial opening to neaten the edges

Pleat Precise fold or series of folds, made in the edge of the fabric to make a longer edge fit a shorter edge

Point turner Tapered tool used to push out points and corners when turning to the right side

Pressing cloth Cloth placed over fabric whilst pressing and ironing to prevent marking or used damp to produce steam

Pressing ham Shaped stuffed cushion used to support fabric whilst pressing curves

Princess seam Seam stitched from the armhole, over the bust and curving into the waistline

Pucker Rippling in the fabric on the stitchline caused by incorrect pinning or stitching

Raglan sleeve Sleeve attached to the garment from the neckline to the underarm by a diagonal seam

Raw edge Fabric edge, which has not been stitched or finished

Reinforcing Stitching over an area again to strengthen - used in areas of most stress

The use of interfacing to strengthen areas of stress in a garment

Reducing bulk Trimming or grading a seam to reduce the thickness of a seam

Right side The side of fabric that will appear on the outside

The side on which the design is printed

Rolled collar Collar that softly rolls and falls away from the neck

Rolled hem Very narrow hem finish

Rotary cutter Cutting tool with a circular blade ideal for cutting long straight lengths of fabric

Rouleau or *tubing*
Narrow tube of fabric

Ruffle or *frill*
Decorative gathered or circular trim

Running stitch Easy hand stitch used to hold layers together or to form decorative stitching

Rolling a seam Bringing a seam to the edge between two layers of fabric, by rolling it backwards and forwards between the thumb and forefinger

Satin stitch Close zigzag stitch which creates a smooth line of close stitching

Seam allowance Width of fabric between the raw edge and the stitchline

Seam ripper Cutting tool designed to rip through stitching when unpicking

Selvedge *(selvage)*
This is the self-finished edge on both sides of the fabric

Set-in sleeve Sleeve stitched into a shaped armhole

Shank Extension at the back of a button to raise it from the fabric

Shirring Rows of machine gathering or narrow elastic used to control fullness

Shoulder pads Felt or foam shaped pads that are inserted into the shoulders of garments to give shape

Sizing Starchy fabric finish used to stiffen and increase bulk

Slash This is an opening cut into the garment

Sleeve head Upper curved section of sleeve, between the marks indicated on the pattern piece

Slipstitch Hemming stitch through a folded edge

Slubs Lumps of fibre in the weave, causing an uneven surface

Spool *or spindle*
The top thread holder on a sewing machine or a reel of thread

Stabiliser Layer of fabric or interfacing applied to the wrong side of the garment piece to provide strength or stability

Staystitch Line of stitching done to stabilise fabric and prevent unwanted stretching prior to seaming - usually placed just inside the stitchline on curved edges

Stay Fabric or tape used to reinforce an area or to prevent stretching

Stitch in the ditch Stitching in the folds between the seam while pulling the fabric tightly from the left and right to expose the seam

Stitchline Line defining the division between seam allowance and garment - the position to place stitching

Tacking *See Basting*

Tailors' tacks Way of marking placement points on garments for buttonholes, darts, pockets etc

Tear-away Easily torn stabiliser - used as temporary firmness behind stitching

Tension Tautness of the machine stitch

On a sewing machine there are two types of tension - thread and bobbin

Toile *or trial*
Rough copy of a garment made from cheaper fabric such as calico, used to ensure good fit before cutting more expensive fabric. Make alterations to the toile, take it apart again and use these pieces as the new pattern

Topstitch Decorative row of stitching, parallel to a seam

Tuck Fold stitched in the fabric and pressed to one side

Trimming Thin decorative strip such as ribbon or lace.

Term used to describe cutting away excess fabric from seam allowances

Turning through Pieces stitched right sides together before turning the right side to face outwards and the seam enclosed within

Twin needle Pair of needle shafts secured into a cross bar extending from a single shank

Underlap The lower section of two overlapping pieces

Underlining Layer of fabric behind the main piece. Provides reinforcement and support to the garment fabric

Understitch Row of stitching through seam allowances and facings, very close to seam - used to stop lining or facings from rolling out

Universal needle The sewing machine needle suited to most sewing tasks

Vent Lined opening allowing for movement when garment is worn

Walking foot Machine presser foot used to provide even tension and feed on the upper surface of the stitching - works in unison with the feed underneath

Warp *or lengthwise grain*
Term describing the yarns running down the length of woven fabric

Weft *or cross grain*
Yarns running at right angles to the lengthwise yarns of woven fabric

Welt Separate fabric strip, often used in the finishing process of a slashed pocket

Wing needle Thick needle with 'wings' at the sides that create holes in the fabric as it stitches

Wrong side Unfinished or less defined side of the fabric inside the garment

Yardage The amount of fabric needed to complete a project for a specific size

Yoke Section of garment that sits flat across the shoulder and neck area or from waist to hip

Zigzag stitch Diagonal machine stitch produced with a side to side movement - used to produce a decorative finish, neaten raw edges or to join two edges butted together

index